www.targettrg.co.uk
www.jcrmjournals.com

Published in 2020 by JCRM Journals, UK

Designed and Produced by Ralph & Claire Moody

Copyright © JCRM Journals & Target Training Associates 2020

All rights reserved. This book and the related brand are protected by copyright. No part of it may be reproduced, stored in a retrieval system, or transmitted in any form or by any other means, without prior permission in writing of the Publisher, nor be otherwise circulated in any form of binding or cover other than that in which it was published.

ISBN: 979-8651912674

Reflection On Your Teaching Skills : Change The Way You Work With Reflection & Action.

Available from Amazon and other leading retail outlets.

If you would like us to create a bespoke journal for your organisation or work role contact us on +44 0800 302 9344.

If you enjoyed this journal please leave us a review on Amazon. Thank you.

www.jcrmjournals.com

Retail enquiries to:
info@targettrg.co.uk

Reflection On Your Teaching Skills

Change the way you work with reflection and action

RALPH & CLAIRE MOODY

www.targettrg.co.uk
www.jcrmjournals.com

In case of loss please return to:

....

....

....

www.targettrg.co.uk
www.jcrmjournals.com

REFLECTION ON YOUR TEACHING SKILLS

CHANGE THE WAY YOU WORK WITH REFLECTION & ACTION.

Our journals are designed to help individuals in any specific area they would like to change in their lives, both professionally and personally. We use coaching questions to guide your thinking in a different way.

When was the last time you reflected on your teaching skills?

A journal is perfect to write your reflections every day. All you need to do is write for five minutes at the beginning or end of every day or both if you choose. Writing in a journal can create significant changes in your life when done correctly. We have both benefitted when writing a journal as do millions of others. It's an excellent opportunity to create a habit and build this into your life and as an example, make it part of your daily routine.

The purpose of this journal is to encourage you to reflect on your teaching skills. To develop into a fantastic teacher not just to be an average teacher, to create a focus for the best development. It's an opportunity to really understand yourself. Our journals are different they look at your thinking around the moments of decision making. It is getting to the route of the problem that creates the change looking past the specifics. We have written specific questions for you to use as a guide; these will help you in particular areas. If you sit with just thinking you will not notice as much as if you write. We felt a 100-day journal to begin with where you put all your reflections together would keep things simple for you. If you force yourself to write every day with your thoughts, you will grow in so many ways. You will be so much more successful in your life if you do this properly. Our aim with this journal is to encourage you to grow and focus to create change. A journal is perfect to record this; keeping all your thoughts and feelings in one place, incredibly powerful and very special.

Try not to make it a tick box exercise, so it becomes a chore. Make it something you look forward to doing, writing your thoughts and feelings on paper so you can reflect and look back. Create the habit and then watch how you develop and grow.

The journal includes a page for every day for you to make notes, then separate reflection sheets for every 10 days and then the final page. Reflection is so critical when writing your journal to see what words keep jumping out. If you find yourself writing the same things recognise this, then think why am I doing this, what change would I like?

Then you can reflect on this and what you can do differently. This will help you think in different ways and what you would like to be different, giving you a focus. Think about how you think and feel, you want to notice differences in yourself to create change, change will be happening if you pay attention.

Forcing yourself to write in a journal will create much more awareness about how you can develop yourself, your mindset and your patterns. There is no doubt you will find yourself improving in your teaching skills. It is little changes that move you to create bigger changes, you have to be committed though.

Writing a journal is an amazing journey, good luck and enjoy the very special thoughts and moments as you watch yourself develop.

Ralph & Claire

Ralph & Claire Moody
Founders of JCRM Journals

HOW TO USE THE JOURNAL

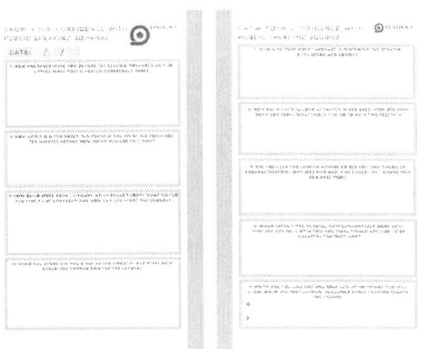

The session sheets are for you to complete each day. Make sure you complete all questions.

Every 10 days complete a review of your actions and reflect on what you have achieved. There is space on the right side for you to make notes.

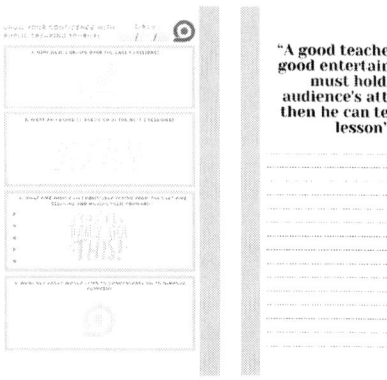

"A good teacher, like a good entertainer first must hold his audience's attention, then he can teach his lesson"

Before we start the journal some pre questions:

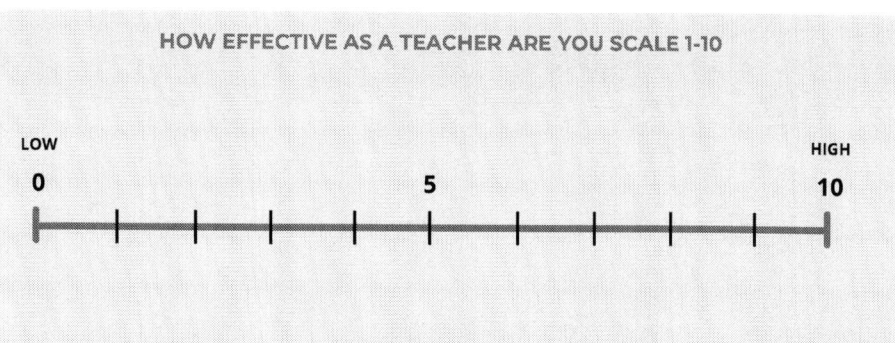

HOW EFFECTIVE AS A TEACHER ARE YOU SCALE 1-10

LOW — 0 — 5 — 10 — HIGH

WHAT WOULD YOU LIKE TO CHANGE WITH YOUR TEACHING, WHAT YOU WOULD LIKE TO BE DIFFERENT ABOUT YOURSELF E.G. APPROACHABLE, ADAPTABLE ETC.?

REFLECTION ON YOUR TEACHING SKILLS - JOURNAL

DAY 1

DATE:-   /   /

1: HOW DISTRACTED DID YOU FIND YOURSELF TODAY WHY WAS THIS? HOW COULD YOU CHANGE THIS FOR THE NEXT LESSON?

2: HOW MOTIVATED WERE YOU TODAY, WHY WAS THIS AND WHAT COULD YOU DO TO IMPROVE THIS?

3: HOW GOOD WERE YOUR COMMUNICATION SKILLS TODAY? WHAT WOULD YOU LIKE TO BE DIFFERENT & HOW CAN YOU START THE CHANGE?

4: WERE YOU PATIENT TODAY? HOW DIFFERENT DO YOU FIND YOURSELF WITH DIFFERENT STUDENTS AND CLASSES? THEN LOOK AT WHY YOU MAY BE DIFFERENT?

REFLECTION ON YOUR TEACHING SKILLS - JOURNAL  DAY 1

5: WERE YOU ABLE TO DEAL WITH ANY CONFLICT TODAY BOTH STUDENTS AND PEERS? VERY USEFUL TO LOOK AT THIS AREA WITHIN YOURSELF AND WHAT YOU COULD DO DIFFERENTLY.

6: HOW ORGANISED WERE YOU TODAY, TOO MUCH OR TOO LITTLE? WHAT WOULD YOU LIKE TO BE DIFFERENT AND HOW YOU ARE GOING TO DEAL WITH THIS DIFFERENTLY?

7: WERE YOU ENTHUSIASTIC TODAY? HOW DID THE CLASS RESPOND TO YOUR ENTHUSIASM? HOW COULD YOU DEVELOP THIS FURTHER?

8: WERE YOU CONFIDENT TODAY, HOW CONFIDENT ARE YOU ALREADY? COULD THIS BE BETTER WITHIN YOUR STUDENTS AND PEERS.

9: HOW SUPPORTIVE HAVE YOU BEEN TODAY, WHY WAS THIS? WHAT IMPROVEMENTS COULD YOU MAKE TO IMPROVE IN THIS AREA?

REFLECTION ON YOUR TEACHING SKILLS - JOURNAL

DAY 2

DATE:-   /   /

1: HOW DISTRACTED DID YOU FIND YOURSELF TODAY WHY WAS THIS? HOW COULD YOU CHANGE THIS FOR THE NEXT LESSON?

2: HOW MOTIVATED WERE YOU TODAY, WHY WAS THIS AND WHAT COULD YOU DO TO IMPROVE THIS?

3: HOW GOOD WERE YOUR COMMUNICATION SKILLS TODAY? WHAT WOULD YOU LIKE TO BE DIFFERENT & HOW CAN YOU START THE CHANGE?

4: WERE YOU PATIENT TODAY? HOW DIFFERENT DO YOU FIND YOURSELF WITH DIFFERENT STUDENTS AND CLASSES? THEN LOOK AT WHY YOU MAY BE DIFFERENT?

REFLECTION ON YOUR TEACHING SKILLS - JOURNAL  DAY 2

5: WERE YOU ABLE TO DEAL WITH ANY CONFLICT TODAY BOTH STUDENTS AND PEERS? VERY USEFUL TO LOOK AT THIS AREA WITHIN YOURSELF AND WHAT YOU COULD DO DIFFERENTLY.

6: HOW ORGANISED WERE YOU TODAY, TOO MUCH OR TOO LITTLE? WHAT WOULD YOU LIKE TO BE DIFFERENT AND HOW YOU ARE GOING TO DEAL WITH THIS DIFFERENTLY?

7: WERE YOU ENTHUSIASTIC TODAY? HOW DID THE CLASS RESPOND TO YOUR ENTHUSIASM? HOW COULD YOU DEVELOP THIS FURTHER?

8: WERE YOU CONFIDENT TODAY, HOW CONFIDENT ARE YOU ALREADY? COULD THIS BE BETTER WITHIN YOUR STUDENTS AND PEERS.

9: HOW SUPPORTIVE HAVE YOU BEEN TODAY, WHY WAS THIS? WHAT IMPROVEMENTS COULD YOU MAKE TO IMPROVE IN THIS AREA?

REFLECTION ON YOUR TEACHING SKILLS - JOURNAL

DAY 3

DATE:-   /   /

1: HOW DISTRACTED DID YOU FIND YOURSELF TODAY WHY WAS THIS? HOW COULD YOU CHANGE THIS FOR THE NEXT LESSON?

2: HOW MOTIVATED WERE YOU TODAY, WHY WAS THIS AND WHAT COULD YOU DO TO IMPROVE THIS?

3: HOW GOOD WERE YOUR COMMUNICATION SKILLS TODAY? WHAT WOULD YOU LIKE TO BE DIFFERENT & HOW CAN YOU START THE CHANGE?

4: WERE YOU PATIENT TODAY? HOW DIFFERENT DO YOU FIND YOURSELF WITH DIFFERENT STUDENTS AND CLASSES? THEN LOOK AT WHY YOU MAY BE DIFFERENT?

REFLECTION ON YOUR TEACHING SKILLS - JOURNAL

 DAY 3

5: WERE YOU ABLE TO DEAL WITH ANY CONFLICT TODAY BOTH STUDENTS AND PEERS? VERY USEFUL TO LOOK AT THIS AREA WITHIN YOURSELF AND WHAT YOU COULD DO DIFFERENTLY.

6: HOW ORGANISED WERE YOU TODAY, TOO MUCH OR TOO LITTLE? WHAT WOULD YOU LIKE TO BE DIFFERENT AND HOW YOU ARE GOING TO DEAL WITH THIS DIFFERENTLY?

7: WERE YOU ENTHUSIASTIC TODAY? HOW DID THE CLASS RESPOND TO YOUR ENTHUSIASM? HOW COULD YOU DEVELOP THIS FURTHER?

8: WERE YOU CONFIDENT TODAY, HOW CONFIDENT ARE YOU ALREADY? COULD THIS BE BETTER WITHIN YOUR STUDENTS AND PEERS.

9: HOW SUPPORTIVE HAVE YOU BEEN TODAY, WHY WAS THIS? WHAT IMPROVEMENTS COULD YOU MAKE TO IMPROVE IN THIS AREA?

REFLECTION ON YOUR TEACHING SKILLS - JOURNAL

DAY 4

DATE:-   /   /

1: HOW DISTRACTED DID YOU FIND YOURSELF TODAY WHY WAS THIS? HOW COULD YOU CHANGE THIS FOR THE NEXT LESSON?

2: HOW MOTIVATED WERE YOU TODAY, WHY WAS THIS AND WHAT COULD YOU DO TO IMPROVE THIS?

3: HOW GOOD WERE YOUR COMMUNICATION SKILLS TODAY? WHAT WOULD YOU LIKE TO BE DIFFERENT & HOW CAN YOU START THE CHANGE?

4: WERE YOU PATIENT TODAY? HOW DIFFERENT DO YOU FIND YOURSELF WITH DIFFERENT STUDENTS AND CLASSES? THEN LOOK AT WHY YOU MAY BE DIFFERENT?

REFLECTION ON YOUR TEACHING SKILLS - JOURNAL

 DAY 4

5: WERE YOU ABLE TO DEAL WITH ANY CONFLICT TODAY BOTH STUDENTS AND PEERS? VERY USEFUL TO LOOK AT THIS AREA WITHIN YOURSELF AND WHAT YOU COULD DO DIFFERENTLY.

6: HOW ORGANISED WERE YOU TODAY, TOO MUCH OR TOO LITTLE? WHAT WOULD YOU LIKE TO BE DIFFERENT AND HOW YOU ARE GOING TO DEAL WITH THIS DIFFERENTLY?

7: WERE YOU ENTHUSIASTIC TODAY? HOW DID THE CLASS RESPOND TO YOUR ENTHUSIASM? HOW COULD YOU DEVELOP THIS FURTHER?

8: WERE YOU CONFIDENT TODAY, HOW CONFIDENT ARE YOU ALREADY? COULD THIS BE BETTER WITHIN YOUR STUDENTS AND PEERS.

9: HOW SUPPORTIVE HAVE YOU BEEN TODAY, WHY WAS THIS? WHAT IMPROVEMENTS COULD YOU MAKE TO IMPROVE IN THIS AREA?

REFLECTION ON YOUR TEACHING SKILLS - JOURNAL

DAY 5

DATE:-   /   /

1: HOW DISTRACTED DID YOU FIND YOURSELF TODAY WHY WAS THIS? HOW COULD YOU CHANGE THIS FOR THE NEXT LESSON?

2: HOW MOTIVATED WERE YOU TODAY, WHY WAS THIS AND WHAT COULD YOU DO TO IMPROVE THIS?

3: HOW GOOD WERE YOUR COMMUNICATION SKILLS TODAY? WHAT WOULD YOU LIKE TO BE DIFFERENT & HOW CAN YOU START THE CHANGE?

4: WERE YOU PATIENT TODAY? HOW DIFFERENT DO YOU FIND YOURSELF WITH DIFFERENT STUDENTS AND CLASSES? THEN LOOK AT WHY YOU MAY BE DIFFERENT?

REFLECTION ON YOUR TEACHING SKILLS - JOURNAL  DAY 5

5: WERE YOU ABLE TO DEAL WITH ANY CONFLICT TODAY BOTH STUDENTS AND PEERS? VERY USEFUL TO LOOK AT THIS AREA WITHIN YOURSELF AND WHAT YOU COULD DO DIFFERENTLY.

6: HOW ORGANISED WERE YOU TODAY, TOO MUCH OR TOO LITTLE? WHAT WOULD YOU LIKE TO BE DIFFERENT AND HOW YOU ARE GOING TO DEAL WITH THIS DIFFERENTLY?

7: WERE YOU ENTHUSIASTIC TODAY? HOW DID THE CLASS RESPOND TO YOUR ENTHUSIASM? HOW COULD YOU DEVELOP THIS FURTHER?

8: WERE YOU CONFIDENT TODAY, HOW CONFIDENT ARE YOU ALREADY? COULD THIS BE BETTER WITHIN YOUR STUDENTS AND PEERS.

9: HOW SUPPORTIVE HAVE YOU BEEN TODAY, WHY WAS THIS? WHAT IMPROVEMENTS COULD YOU MAKE TO IMPROVE IN THIS AREA?

REFLECTION ON YOUR TEACHING SKILLS - JOURNAL

DAY 6

DATE:-   /   /

1: HOW DISTRACTED DID YOU FIND YOURSELF TODAY WHY WAS THIS? HOW COULD YOU CHANGE THIS FOR THE NEXT LESSON?

2: HOW MOTIVATED WERE YOU TODAY, WHY WAS THIS AND WHAT COULD YOU DO TO IMPROVE THIS?

3: HOW GOOD WERE YOUR COMMUNICATION SKILLS TODAY? WHAT WOULD YOU LIKE TO BE DIFFERENT & HOW CAN YOU START THE CHANGE?

4: WERE YOU PATIENT TODAY? HOW DIFFERENT DO YOU FIND YOURSELF WITH DIFFERENT STUDENTS AND CLASSES? THEN LOOK AT WHY YOU MAY BE DIFFERENT?

REFLECTION ON YOUR TEACHING SKILLS - JOURNAL  DAY 6

5: WERE YOU ABLE TO DEAL WITH ANY CONFLICT TODAY BOTH STUDENTS AND PEERS? VERY USEFUL TO LOOK AT THIS AREA WITHIN YOURSELF AND WHAT YOU COULD DO DIFFERENTLY.

6: HOW ORGANISED WERE YOU TODAY, TOO MUCH OR TOO LITTLE? WHAT WOULD YOU LIKE TO BE DIFFERENT AND HOW YOU ARE GOING TO DEAL WITH THIS DIFFERENTLY?

7: WERE YOU ENTHUSIASTIC TODAY? HOW DID THE CLASS RESPOND TO YOUR ENTHUSIASM? HOW COULD YOU DEVELOP THIS FURTHER?

8: WERE YOU CONFIDENT TODAY, HOW CONFIDENT ARE YOU ALREADY? COULD THIS BE BETTER WITHIN YOUR STUDENTS AND PEERS.

9: HOW SUPPORTIVE HAVE YOU BEEN TODAY, WHY WAS THIS? WHAT IMPROVEMENTS COULD YOU MAKE TO IMPROVE IN THIS AREA?

REFLECTION ON YOUR TEACHING SKILLS - JOURNAL

DAY 7

DATE:-   /   /

1: HOW DISTRACTED DID YOU FIND YOURSELF TODAY WHY WAS THIS? HOW COULD YOU CHANGE THIS FOR THE NEXT LESSON?

2: HOW MOTIVATED WERE YOU TODAY, WHY WAS THIS AND WHAT COULD YOU DO TO IMPROVE THIS?

3: HOW GOOD WERE YOUR COMMUNICATION SKILLS TODAY? WHAT WOULD YOU LIKE TO BE DIFFERENT & HOW CAN YOU START THE CHANGE?

4: WERE YOU PATIENT TODAY? HOW DIFFERENT DO YOU FIND YOURSELF WITH DIFFERENT STUDENTS AND CLASSES? THEN LOOK AT WHY YOU MAY BE DIFFERENT?

REFLECTION ON YOUR TEACHING SKILLS - JOURNAL

 DAY 7

5: WERE YOU ABLE TO DEAL WITH ANY CONFLICT TODAY BOTH STUDENTS AND PEERS? VERY USEFUL TO LOOK AT THIS AREA WITHIN YOURSELF AND WHAT YOU COULD DO DIFFERENTLY.

6: HOW ORGANISED WERE YOU TODAY, TOO MUCH OR TOO LITTLE? WHAT WOULD YOU LIKE TO BE DIFFERENT AND HOW YOU ARE GOING TO DEAL WITH THIS DIFFERENTLY?

7: WERE YOU ENTHUSIASTIC TODAY? HOW DID THE CLASS RESPOND TO YOUR ENTHUSIASM? HOW COULD YOU DEVELOP THIS FURTHER?

8: WERE YOU CONFIDENT TODAY, HOW CONFIDENT ARE YOU ALREADY? COULD THIS BE BETTER WITHIN YOUR STUDENTS AND PEERS.

9: HOW SUPPORTIVE HAVE YOU BEEN TODAY, WHY WAS THIS? WHAT IMPROVEMENTS COULD YOU MAKE TO IMPROVE IN THIS AREA?

REFLECTION ON YOUR TEACHING SKILLS - JOURNAL

DAY 8

DATE:-   /   /

1: HOW DISTRACTED DID YOU FIND YOURSELF TODAY WHY WAS THIS? HOW COULD YOU CHANGE THIS FOR THE NEXT LESSON?

2: HOW MOTIVATED WERE YOU TODAY, WHY WAS THIS AND WHAT COULD YOU DO TO IMPROVE THIS?

3: HOW GOOD WERE YOUR COMMUNICATION SKILLS TODAY? WHAT WOULD YOU LIKE TO BE DIFFERENT & HOW CAN YOU START THE CHANGE?

4: WERE YOU PATIENT TODAY? HOW DIFFERENT DO YOU FIND YOURSELF WITH DIFFERENT STUDENTS AND CLASSES? THEN LOOK AT WHY YOU MAY BE DIFFERENT?

REFLECTION ON YOUR TEACHING SKILLS - JOURNAL  DAY 8

5: WERE YOU ABLE TO DEAL WITH ANY CONFLICT TODAY BOTH STUDENTS AND PEERS? VERY USEFUL TO LOOK AT THIS AREA WITHIN YOURSELF AND WHAT YOU COULD DO DIFFERENTLY.

6: HOW ORGANISED WERE YOU TODAY, TOO MUCH OR TOO LITTLE? WHAT WOULD YOU LIKE TO BE DIFFERENT AND HOW YOU ARE GOING TO DEAL WITH THIS DIFFERENTLY?

7: WERE YOU ENTHUSIASTIC TODAY? HOW DID THE CLASS RESPOND TO YOUR ENTHUSIASM? HOW COULD YOU DEVELOP THIS FURTHER?

8: WERE YOU CONFIDENT TODAY, HOW CONFIDENT ARE YOU ALREADY? COULD THIS BE BETTER WITHIN YOUR STUDENTS AND PEERS.

9: HOW SUPPORTIVE HAVE YOU BEEN TODAY, WHY WAS THIS? WHAT IMPROVEMENTS COULD YOU MAKE TO IMPROVE IN THIS AREA?

REFLECTION ON YOUR TEACHING SKILLS - JOURNAL

DAY 9

DATE:-   /   /

1: HOW DISTRACTED DID YOU FIND YOURSELF TODAY WHY WAS THIS? HOW COULD YOU CHANGE THIS FOR THE NEXT LESSON?

2: HOW MOTIVATED WERE YOU TODAY, WHY WAS THIS AND WHAT COULD YOU DO TO IMPROVE THIS?

3: HOW GOOD WERE YOUR COMMUNICATION SKILLS TODAY? WHAT WOULD YOU LIKE TO BE DIFFERENT & HOW CAN YOU START THE CHANGE?

4: WERE YOU PATIENT TODAY? HOW DIFFERENT DO YOU FIND YOURSELF WITH DIFFERENT STUDENTS AND CLASSES? THEN LOOK AT WHY YOU MAY BE DIFFERENT?

REFLECTION ON YOUR TEACHING SKILLS - JOURNAL

 DAY 9

5: WERE YOU ABLE TO DEAL WITH ANY CONFLICT TODAY BOTH STUDENTS AND PEERS? VERY USEFUL TO LOOK AT THIS AREA WITHIN YOURSELF AND WHAT YOU COULD DO DIFFERENTLY.

6: HOW ORGANISED WERE YOU TODAY, TOO MUCH OR TOO LITTLE? WHAT WOULD YOU LIKE TO BE DIFFERENT AND HOW YOU ARE GOING TO DEAL WITH THIS DIFFERENTLY?

7: WERE YOU ENTHUSIASTIC TODAY? HOW DID THE CLASS RESPOND TO YOUR ENTHUSIASM? HOW COULD YOU DEVELOP THIS FURTHER?

8: WERE YOU CONFIDENT TODAY, HOW CONFIDENT ARE YOU ALREADY? COULD THIS BE BETTER WITHIN YOUR STUDENTS AND PEERS.

9: HOW SUPPORTIVE HAVE YOU BEEN TODAY, WHY WAS THIS? WHAT IMPROVEMENTS COULD YOU MAKE TO IMPROVE IN THIS AREA?

REFLECTION ON YOUR TEACHING SKILLS - JOURNAL

DAY 10

DATE:-   /   /

1: HOW DISTRACTED DID YOU FIND YOURSELF TODAY WHY WAS THIS? HOW COULD YOU CHANGE THIS FOR THE NEXT LESSON?

2: HOW MOTIVATED WERE YOU TODAY, WHY WAS THIS AND WHAT COULD YOU DO TO IMPROVE THIS?

3: HOW GOOD WERE YOUR COMMUNICATION SKILLS TODAY? WHAT WOULD YOU LIKE TO BE DIFFERENT & HOW CAN YOU START THE CHANGE?

4: WERE YOU PATIENT TODAY? HOW DIFFERENT DO YOU FIND YOURSELF WITH DIFFERENT STUDENTS AND CLASSES? THEN LOOK AT WHY YOU MAY BE DIFFERENT?

REFLECTION ON YOUR TEACHING SKILLS - JOURNAL

5: WERE YOU ABLE TO DEAL WITH ANY CONFLICT TODAY BOTH STUDENTS AND PEERS? VERY USEFUL TO LOOK AT THIS AREA WITHIN YOURSELF AND WHAT YOU COULD DO DIFFERENTLY.

6: HOW ORGANISED WERE YOU TODAY, TOO MUCH OR TOO LITTLE? WHAT WOULD YOU LIKE TO BE DIFFERENT AND HOW YOU ARE GOING TO DEAL WITH THIS DIFFERENTLY?

7: WERE YOU ENTHUSIASTIC TODAY? HOW DID THE CLASS RESPOND TO YOUR ENTHUSIASM? HOW COULD YOU DEVELOP THIS FURTHER?

8: WERE YOU CONFIDENT TODAY, HOW CONFIDENT ARE YOU ALREADY? COULD THIS BE BETTER WITHIN YOUR STUDENTS AND PEERS.

9: HOW SUPPORTIVE HAVE YOU BEEN TODAY, WHY WAS THIS? WHAT IMPROVEMENTS COULD YOU MAKE TO IMPROVE IN THIS AREA?

REFLECTION ON YOUR TEACHING SKILLS - JOURNAL

DAY 1 - 10 REVIEW

1: HOW HAVE I GROWN OVER THE LAST 10 DAYS?

2: WHAT AM I GOING TO FOCUS ON OVER THE NEXT 10 DAYS?

3: WHAT FIVE THINGS AM I POSITIVELY TAKING FROM THE LAST 10 DAYS AND MOVING THEM FORWARD INTO THE NEXT 10 DAYS.

-
-
-
-
-

4: WHAT KEY AREAS WOULD I LIKE TO CONCENTRATE ON TO IMPROVE MY TEACHING SKILLS FURTHER?

> "A good teacher, like a good entertainer first must hold his audience's attention, then he can teach his lesson"

REFLECTION ON YOUR TEACHING SKILLS - JOURNAL

DAY 11

DATE:-   /   /

1: HOW DISTRACTED DID YOU FIND YOURSELF TODAY WHY WAS THIS? HOW COULD YOU CHANGE THIS FOR THE NEXT LESSON?

2: HOW MOTIVATED WERE YOU TODAY, WHY WAS THIS AND WHAT COULD YOU DO TO IMPROVE THIS?

3: HOW GOOD WERE YOUR COMMUNICATION SKILLS TODAY? WHAT WOULD YOU LIKE TO BE DIFFERENT & HOW CAN YOU START THE CHANGE?

4: WERE YOU PATIENT TODAY? HOW DIFFERENT DO YOU FIND YOURSELF WITH DIFFERENT STUDENTS AND CLASSES? THEN LOOK AT WHY YOU MAY BE DIFFERENT?

REFLECTION ON YOUR TEACHING SKILLS - JOURNAL

 DAY 11

5: WERE YOU ABLE TO DEAL WITH ANY CONFLICT TODAY BOTH STUDENTS AND PEERS? VERY USEFUL TO LOOK AT THIS AREA WITHIN YOURSELF AND WHAT YOU COULD DO DIFFERENTLY.

6: HOW ORGANISED WERE YOU TODAY, TOO MUCH OR TOO LITTLE? WHAT WOULD YOU LIKE TO BE DIFFERENT AND HOW YOU ARE GOING TO DEAL WITH THIS DIFFERENTLY?

7: WERE YOU ENTHUSIASTIC TODAY? HOW DID THE CLASS RESPOND TO YOUR ENTHUSIASM? HOW COULD YOU DEVELOP THIS FURTHER?

8: WERE YOU CONFIDENT TODAY, HOW CONFIDENT ARE YOU ALREADY? COULD THIS BE BETTER WITHIN YOUR STUDENTS AND PEERS.

9: HOW SUPPORTIVE HAVE YOU BEEN TODAY, WHY WAS THIS? WHAT IMPROVEMENTS COULD YOU MAKE TO IMPROVE IN THIS AREA?

REFLECTION ON YOUR TEACHING SKILLS - JOURNAL

DAY 12

DATE:-   /   /

1: HOW DISTRACTED DID YOU FIND YOURSELF TODAY WHY WAS THIS? HOW COULD YOU CHANGE THIS FOR THE NEXT LESSON?

2: HOW MOTIVATED WERE YOU TODAY, WHY WAS THIS AND WHAT COULD YOU DO TO IMPROVE THIS?

3: HOW GOOD WERE YOUR COMMUNICATION SKILLS TODAY? WHAT WOULD YOU LIKE TO BE DIFFERENT & HOW CAN YOU START THE CHANGE?

4: WERE YOU PATIENT TODAY? HOW DIFFERENT DO YOU FIND YOURSELF WITH DIFFERENT STUDENTS AND CLASSES? THEN LOOK AT WHY YOU MAY BE DIFFERENT?

REFLECTION ON YOUR TEACHING SKILLS - JOURNAL

 DAY 12

5: WERE YOU ABLE TO DEAL WITH ANY CONFLICT TODAY BOTH STUDENTS AND PEERS? VERY USEFUL TO LOOK AT THIS AREA WITHIN YOURSELF AND WHAT YOU COULD DO DIFFERENTLY.

6: HOW ORGANISED WERE YOU TODAY, TOO MUCH OR TOO LITTLE? WHAT WOULD YOU LIKE TO BE DIFFERENT AND HOW YOU ARE GOING TO DEAL WITH THIS DIFFERENTLY?

7: WERE YOU ENTHUSIASTIC TODAY? HOW DID THE CLASS RESPOND TO YOUR ENTHUSIASM? HOW COULD YOU DEVELOP THIS FURTHER?

8: WERE YOU CONFIDENT TODAY, HOW CONFIDENT ARE YOU ALREADY? COULD THIS BE BETTER WITHIN YOUR STUDENTS AND PEERS.

9: HOW SUPPORTIVE HAVE YOU BEEN TODAY, WHY WAS THIS? WHAT IMPROVEMENTS COULD YOU MAKE TO IMPROVE IN THIS AREA?

REFLECTION ON YOUR TEACHING SKILLS - JOURNAL

DAY 13

DATE:-   /   /

1: HOW DISTRACTED DID YOU FIND YOURSELF TODAY WHY WAS THIS? HOW COULD YOU CHANGE THIS FOR THE NEXT LESSON?

2: HOW MOTIVATED WERE YOU TODAY, WHY WAS THIS AND WHAT COULD YOU DO TO IMPROVE THIS?

3: HOW GOOD WERE YOUR COMMUNICATION SKILLS TODAY? WHAT WOULD YOU LIKE TO BE DIFFERENT & HOW CAN YOU START THE CHANGE?

4: WERE YOU PATIENT TODAY? HOW DIFFERENT DO YOU FIND YOURSELF WITH DIFFERENT STUDENTS AND CLASSES? THEN LOOK AT WHY YOU MAY BE DIFFERENT?

REFLECTION ON YOUR TEACHING SKILLS - JOURNAL

 DAY 13

5: WERE YOU ABLE TO DEAL WITH ANY CONFLICT TODAY BOTH STUDENTS AND PEERS? VERY USEFUL TO LOOK AT THIS AREA WITHIN YOURSELF AND WHAT YOU COULD DO DIFFERENTLY.

6: HOW ORGANISED WERE YOU TODAY, TOO MUCH OR TOO LITTLE? WHAT WOULD YOU LIKE TO BE DIFFERENT AND HOW YOU ARE GOING TO DEAL WITH THIS DIFFERENTLY?

7: WERE YOU ENTHUSIASTIC TODAY? HOW DID THE CLASS RESPOND TO YOUR ENTHUSIASM? HOW COULD YOU DEVELOP THIS FURTHER?

8: WERE YOU CONFIDENT TODAY, HOW CONFIDENT ARE YOU ALREADY? COULD THIS BE BETTER WITHIN YOUR STUDENTS AND PEERS.

9: HOW SUPPORTIVE HAVE YOU BEEN TODAY, WHY WAS THIS? WHAT IMPROVEMENTS COULD YOU MAKE TO IMPROVE IN THIS AREA?

REFLECTION ON YOUR TEACHING SKILLS - JOURNAL

DAY 14

DATE:-   /   /

1: HOW DISTRACTED DID YOU FIND YOURSELF TODAY WHY WAS THIS? HOW COULD YOU CHANGE THIS FOR THE NEXT LESSON?

2: HOW MOTIVATED WERE YOU TODAY, WHY WAS THIS AND WHAT COULD YOU DO TO IMPROVE THIS?

3: HOW GOOD WERE YOUR COMMUNICATION SKILLS TODAY? WHAT WOULD YOU LIKE TO BE DIFFERENT & HOW CAN YOU START THE CHANGE?

4: WERE YOU PATIENT TODAY? HOW DIFFERENT DO YOU FIND YOURSELF WITH DIFFERENT STUDENTS AND CLASSES? THEN LOOK AT WHY YOU MAY BE DIFFERENT?

REFLECTION ON YOUR TEACHING SKILLS - JOURNAL

5: WERE YOU ABLE TO DEAL WITH ANY CONFLICT TODAY BOTH STUDENTS AND PEERS? VERY USEFUL TO LOOK AT THIS AREA WITHIN YOURSELF AND WHAT YOU COULD DO DIFFERENTLY.

6: HOW ORGANISED WERE YOU TODAY, TOO MUCH OR TOO LITTLE? WHAT WOULD YOU LIKE TO BE DIFFERENT AND HOW YOU ARE GOING TO DEAL WITH THIS DIFFERENTLY?

7: WERE YOU ENTHUSIASTIC TODAY? HOW DID THE CLASS RESPOND TO YOUR ENTHUSIASM? HOW COULD YOU DEVELOP THIS FURTHER?

8: WERE YOU CONFIDENT TODAY, HOW CONFIDENT ARE YOU ALREADY? COULD THIS BE BETTER WITHIN YOUR STUDENTS AND PEERS.

9: HOW SUPPORTIVE HAVE YOU BEEN TODAY, WHY WAS THIS? WHAT IMPROVEMENTS COULD YOU MAKE TO IMPROVE IN THIS AREA?

REFLECTION ON YOUR TEACHING SKILLS - JOURNAL

DAY 15

DATE:-   /   /

1: HOW DISTRACTED DID YOU FIND YOURSELF TODAY WHY WAS THIS? HOW COULD YOU CHANGE THIS FOR THE NEXT LESSON?

2: HOW MOTIVATED WERE YOU TODAY, WHY WAS THIS AND WHAT COULD YOU DO TO IMPROVE THIS?

3: HOW GOOD WERE YOUR COMMUNICATION SKILLS TODAY? WHAT WOULD YOU LIKE TO BE DIFFERENT & HOW CAN YOU START THE CHANGE?

4: WERE YOU PATIENT TODAY? HOW DIFFERENT DO YOU FIND YOURSELF WITH DIFFERENT STUDENTS AND CLASSES? THEN LOOK AT WHY YOU MAY BE DIFFERENT?

REFLECTION ON YOUR TEACHING SKILLS - JOURNAL

 DAY 15

5: WERE YOU ABLE TO DEAL WITH ANY CONFLICT TODAY BOTH STUDENTS AND PEERS? VERY USEFUL TO LOOK AT THIS AREA WITHIN YOURSELF AND WHAT YOU COULD DO DIFFERENTLY.

6: HOW ORGANISED WERE YOU TODAY, TOO MUCH OR TOO LITTLE? WHAT WOULD YOU LIKE TO BE DIFFERENT AND HOW YOU ARE GOING TO DEAL WITH THIS DIFFERENTLY?

7: WERE YOU ENTHUSIASTIC TODAY? HOW DID THE CLASS RESPOND TO YOUR ENTHUSIASM? HOW COULD YOU DEVELOP THIS FURTHER?

8: WERE YOU CONFIDENT TODAY, HOW CONFIDENT ARE YOU ALREADY? COULD THIS BE BETTER WITHIN YOUR STUDENTS AND PEERS.

9: HOW SUPPORTIVE HAVE YOU BEEN TODAY, WHY WAS THIS? WHAT IMPROVEMENTS COULD YOU MAKE TO IMPROVE IN THIS AREA?

REFLECTION ON YOUR TEACHING SKILLS - JOURNAL

DAY 16

DATE:-   /   /

1: HOW DISTRACTED DID YOU FIND YOURSELF TODAY WHY WAS THIS? HOW COULD YOU CHANGE THIS FOR THE NEXT LESSON?

2: HOW MOTIVATED WERE YOU TODAY, WHY WAS THIS AND WHAT COULD YOU DO TO IMPROVE THIS?

3: HOW GOOD WERE YOUR COMMUNICATION SKILLS TODAY? WHAT WOULD YOU LIKE TO BE DIFFERENT & HOW CAN YOU START THE CHANGE?

4: WERE YOU PATIENT TODAY? HOW DIFFERENT DO YOU FIND YOURSELF WITH DIFFERENT STUDENTS AND CLASSES? THEN LOOK AT WHY YOU MAY BE DIFFERENT?

REFLECTION ON YOUR TEACHING SKILLS - JOURNAL

 DAY 16

5: WERE YOU ABLE TO DEAL WITH ANY CONFLICT TODAY BOTH STUDENTS AND PEERS? VERY USEFUL TO LOOK AT THIS AREA WITHIN YOURSELF AND WHAT YOU COULD DO DIFFERENTLY.

6: HOW ORGANISED WERE YOU TODAY, TOO MUCH OR TOO LITTLE? WHAT WOULD YOU LIKE TO BE DIFFERENT AND HOW YOU ARE GOING TO DEAL WITH THIS DIFFERENTLY?

7: WERE YOU ENTHUSIASTIC TODAY? HOW DID THE CLASS RESPOND TO YOUR ENTHUSIASM? HOW COULD YOU DEVELOP THIS FURTHER?

8: WERE YOU CONFIDENT TODAY, HOW CONFIDENT ARE YOU ALREADY? COULD THIS BE BETTER WITHIN YOUR STUDENTS AND PEERS.

9: HOW SUPPORTIVE HAVE YOU BEEN TODAY, WHY WAS THIS? WHAT IMPROVEMENTS COULD YOU MAKE TO IMPROVE IN THIS AREA?

REFLECTION ON YOUR TEACHING SKILLS - JOURNAL

DAY 17

DATE:-   /   /

1: HOW DISTRACTED DID YOU FIND YOURSELF TODAY WHY WAS THIS? HOW COULD YOU CHANGE THIS FOR THE NEXT LESSON?

2: HOW MOTIVATED WERE YOU TODAY, WHY WAS THIS AND WHAT COULD YOU DO TO IMPROVE THIS?

3: HOW GOOD WERE YOUR COMMUNICATION SKILLS TODAY? WHAT WOULD YOU LIKE TO BE DIFFERENT & HOW CAN YOU START THE CHANGE?

4: WERE YOU PATIENT TODAY? HOW DIFFERENT DO YOU FIND YOURSELF WITH DIFFERENT STUDENTS AND CLASSES? THEN LOOK AT WHY YOU MAY BE DIFFERENT?

REFLECTION ON YOUR TEACHING SKILLS - JOURNAL

 DAY 17

5: WERE YOU ABLE TO DEAL WITH ANY CONFLICT TODAY BOTH STUDENTS AND PEERS? VERY USEFUL TO LOOK AT THIS AREA WITHIN YOURSELF AND WHAT YOU COULD DO DIFFERENTLY.

6: HOW ORGANISED WERE YOU TODAY, TOO MUCH OR TOO LITTLE? WHAT WOULD YOU LIKE TO BE DIFFERENT AND HOW YOU ARE GOING TO DEAL WITH THIS DIFFERENTLY?

7: WERE YOU ENTHUSIASTIC TODAY? HOW DID THE CLASS RESPOND TO YOUR ENTHUSIASM? HOW COULD YOU DEVELOP THIS FURTHER?

8: WERE YOU CONFIDENT TODAY, HOW CONFIDENT ARE YOU ALREADY? COULD THIS BE BETTER WITHIN YOUR STUDENTS AND PEERS.

9: HOW SUPPORTIVE HAVE YOU BEEN TODAY, WHY WAS THIS? WHAT IMPROVEMENTS COULD YOU MAKE TO IMPROVE IN THIS AREA?

REFLECTION ON YOUR TEACHING SKILLS - JOURNAL

DAY 18

DATE:-   /   /

1: HOW DISTRACTED DID YOU FIND YOURSELF TODAY WHY WAS THIS? HOW COULD YOU CHANGE THIS FOR THE NEXT LESSON?

2: HOW MOTIVATED WERE YOU TODAY, WHY WAS THIS AND WHAT COULD YOU DO TO IMPROVE THIS?

3: HOW GOOD WERE YOUR COMMUNICATION SKILLS TODAY? WHAT WOULD YOU LIKE TO BE DIFFERENT & HOW CAN YOU START THE CHANGE?

4: WERE YOU PATIENT TODAY? HOW DIFFERENT DO YOU FIND YOURSELF WITH DIFFERENT STUDENTS AND CLASSES? THEN LOOK AT WHY YOU MAY BE DIFFERENT?

REFLECTION ON YOUR TEACHING SKILLS - JOURNAL

 DAY 18

5: WERE YOU ABLE TO DEAL WITH ANY CONFLICT TODAY BOTH STUDENTS AND PEERS? VERY USEFUL TO LOOK AT THIS AREA WITHIN YOURSELF AND WHAT YOU COULD DO DIFFERENTLY.

6: HOW ORGANISED WERE YOU TODAY, TOO MUCH OR TOO LITTLE? WHAT WOULD YOU LIKE TO BE DIFFERENT AND HOW YOU ARE GOING TO DEAL WITH THIS DIFFERENTLY?

7: WERE YOU ENTHUSIASTIC TODAY? HOW DID THE CLASS RESPOND TO YOUR ENTHUSIASM? HOW COULD YOU DEVELOP THIS FURTHER?

8: WERE YOU CONFIDENT TODAY, HOW CONFIDENT ARE YOU ALREADY? COULD THIS BE BETTER WITHIN YOUR STUDENTS AND PEERS.

9: HOW SUPPORTIVE HAVE YOU BEEN TODAY, WHY WAS THIS? WHAT IMPROVEMENTS COULD YOU MAKE TO IMPROVE IN THIS AREA?

REFLECTION ON YOUR TEACHING SKILLS - JOURNAL

DAY 19

DATE:-   /   /

1: HOW DISTRACTED DID YOU FIND YOURSELF TODAY WHY WAS THIS? HOW COULD YOU CHANGE THIS FOR THE NEXT LESSON?

2: HOW MOTIVATED WERE YOU TODAY, WHY WAS THIS AND WHAT COULD YOU DO TO IMPROVE THIS?

3: HOW GOOD WERE YOUR COMMUNICATION SKILLS TODAY? WHAT WOULD YOU LIKE TO BE DIFFERENT & HOW CAN YOU START THE CHANGE?

4: WERE YOU PATIENT TODAY? HOW DIFFERENT DO YOU FIND YOURSELF WITH DIFFERENT STUDENTS AND CLASSES? THEN LOOK AT WHY YOU MAY BE DIFFERENT?

REFLECTION ON YOUR TEACHING SKILLS - JOURNAL

 DAY 19

5: WERE YOU ABLE TO DEAL WITH ANY CONFLICT TODAY BOTH STUDENTS AND PEERS? VERY USEFUL TO LOOK AT THIS AREA WITHIN YOURSELF AND WHAT YOU COULD DO DIFFERENTLY.

6: HOW ORGANISED WERE YOU TODAY, TOO MUCH OR TOO LITTLE? WHAT WOULD YOU LIKE TO BE DIFFERENT AND HOW YOU ARE GOING TO DEAL WITH THIS DIFFERENTLY?

7: WERE YOU ENTHUSIASTIC TODAY? HOW DID THE CLASS RESPOND TO YOUR ENTHUSIASM? HOW COULD YOU DEVELOP THIS FURTHER?

8: WERE YOU CONFIDENT TODAY, HOW CONFIDENT ARE YOU ALREADY? COULD THIS BE BETTER WITHIN YOUR STUDENTS AND PEERS.

9: HOW SUPPORTIVE HAVE YOU BEEN TODAY, WHY WAS THIS? WHAT IMPROVEMENTS COULD YOU MAKE TO IMPROVE IN THIS AREA?

REFLECTION ON YOUR TEACHING SKILLS - JOURNAL

DAY 20

DATE:-   /   /

1: HOW DISTRACTED DID YOU FIND YOURSELF TODAY WHY WAS THIS? HOW COULD YOU CHANGE THIS FOR THE NEXT LESSON?

2: HOW MOTIVATED WERE YOU TODAY, WHY WAS THIS AND WHAT COULD YOU DO TO IMPROVE THIS?

3: HOW GOOD WERE YOUR COMMUNICATION SKILLS TODAY? WHAT WOULD YOU LIKE TO BE DIFFERENT & HOW CAN YOU START THE CHANGE?

4: WERE YOU PATIENT TODAY? HOW DIFFERENT DO YOU FIND YOURSELF WITH DIFFERENT STUDENTS AND CLASSES? THEN LOOK AT WHY YOU MAY BE DIFFERENT?

REFLECTION ON YOUR TEACHING SKILLS - JOURNAL

 DAY 20

5: WERE YOU ABLE TO DEAL WITH ANY CONFLICT TODAY BOTH STUDENTS AND PEERS? VERY USEFUL TO LOOK AT THIS AREA WITHIN YOURSELF AND WHAT YOU COULD DO DIFFERENTLY.

6: HOW ORGANISED WERE YOU TODAY, TOO MUCH OR TOO LITTLE? WHAT WOULD YOU LIKE TO BE DIFFERENT AND HOW YOU ARE GOING TO DEAL WITH THIS DIFFERENTLY?

7: WERE YOU ENTHUSIASTIC TODAY? HOW DID THE CLASS RESPOND TO YOUR ENTHUSIASM? HOW COULD YOU DEVELOP THIS FURTHER?

8: WERE YOU CONFIDENT TODAY, HOW CONFIDENT ARE YOU ALREADY? COULD THIS BE BETTER WITHIN YOUR STUDENTS AND PEERS.

9: HOW SUPPORTIVE HAVE YOU BEEN TODAY, WHY WAS THIS? WHAT IMPROVEMENTS COULD YOU MAKE TO IMPROVE IN THIS AREA?

REFLECTION ON YOUR TEACHING SKILLS - JOURNAL

DAY 11 - 20 REVIEW

1: HOW HAVE I GROWN OVER THE LAST 10 DAYS?

2: WHAT AM I GOING TO FOCUS ON OVER THE NEXT 10 DAYS?

3: WHAT FIVE THINGS AM I POSITIVELY TAKING FROM THE LAST 10 DAYS AND MOVING THEM FORWARD INTO THE NEXT 10 DAYS.

-
-
-
-
-

4: WHAT KEY AREAS WOULD I LIKE TO CONCENTRATE ON TO IMPROVE MY TEACHING SKILLS FURTHER?

"The mediocre teacher tells. The good teacher explains. The superior teacher demonstrates. The great teacher inspires."

REFLECTION ON YOUR TEACHING SKILLS - JOURNAL

DAY 21

DATE:-   /   /

1: HOW DISTRACTED DID YOU FIND YOURSELF TODAY WHY WAS THIS? HOW COULD YOU CHANGE THIS FOR THE NEXT LESSON?

2: HOW MOTIVATED WERE YOU TODAY, WHY WAS THIS AND WHAT COULD YOU DO TO IMPROVE THIS?

3: HOW GOOD WERE YOUR COMMUNICATION SKILLS TODAY? WHAT WOULD YOU LIKE TO BE DIFFERENT & HOW CAN YOU START THE CHANGE?

4: WERE YOU PATIENT TODAY? HOW DIFFERENT DO YOU FIND YOURSELF WITH DIFFERENT STUDENTS AND CLASSES? THEN LOOK AT WHY YOU MAY BE DIFFERENT?

REFLECTION ON YOUR TEACHING SKILLS - JOURNAL

 DAY 21

5: WERE YOU ABLE TO DEAL WITH ANY CONFLICT TODAY BOTH STUDENTS AND PEERS? VERY USEFUL TO LOOK AT THIS AREA WITHIN YOURSELF AND WHAT YOU COULD DO DIFFERENTLY.

6: HOW ORGANISED WERE YOU TODAY, TOO MUCH OR TOO LITTLE? WHAT WOULD YOU LIKE TO BE DIFFERENT AND HOW YOU ARE GOING TO DEAL WITH THIS DIFFERENTLY?

7: WERE YOU ENTHUSIASTIC TODAY? HOW DID THE CLASS RESPOND TO YOUR ENTHUSIASM? HOW COULD YOU DEVELOP THIS FURTHER?

8: WERE YOU CONFIDENT TODAY, HOW CONFIDENT ARE YOU ALREADY? COULD THIS BE BETTER WITHIN YOUR STUDENTS AND PEERS.

9: HOW SUPPORTIVE HAVE YOU BEEN TODAY, WHY WAS THIS? WHAT IMPROVEMENTS COULD YOU MAKE TO IMPROVE IN THIS AREA?

REFLECTION ON YOUR TEACHING SKILLS - JOURNAL

DAY 22

DATE:-   /   /

1: HOW DISTRACTED DID YOU FIND YOURSELF TODAY WHY WAS THIS? HOW COULD YOU CHANGE THIS FOR THE NEXT LESSON?

2: HOW MOTIVATED WERE YOU TODAY, WHY WAS THIS AND WHAT COULD YOU DO TO IMPROVE THIS?

3: HOW GOOD WERE YOUR COMMUNICATION SKILLS TODAY? WHAT WOULD YOU LIKE TO BE DIFFERENT & HOW CAN YOU START THE CHANGE?

4: WERE YOU PATIENT TODAY? HOW DIFFERENT DO YOU FIND YOURSELF WITH DIFFERENT STUDENTS AND CLASSES? THEN LOOK AT WHY YOU MAY BE DIFFERENT?

REFLECTION ON YOUR TEACHING SKILLS - JOURNAL

 DAY 22

5: WERE YOU ABLE TO DEAL WITH ANY CONFLICT TODAY BOTH STUDENTS AND PEERS? VERY USEFUL TO LOOK AT THIS AREA WITHIN YOURSELF AND WHAT YOU COULD DO DIFFERENTLY.

6: HOW ORGANISED WERE YOU TODAY, TOO MUCH OR TOO LITTLE? WHAT WOULD YOU LIKE TO BE DIFFERENT AND HOW YOU ARE GOING TO DEAL WITH THIS DIFFERENTLY?

7: WERE YOU ENTHUSIASTIC TODAY? HOW DID THE CLASS RESPOND TO YOUR ENTHUSIASM? HOW COULD YOU DEVELOP THIS FURTHER?

8: WERE YOU CONFIDENT TODAY, HOW CONFIDENT ARE YOU ALREADY? COULD THIS BE BETTER WITHIN YOUR STUDENTS AND PEERS.

9: HOW SUPPORTIVE HAVE YOU BEEN TODAY, WHY WAS THIS? WHAT IMPROVEMENTS COULD YOU MAKE TO IMPROVE IN THIS AREA?

REFLECTION ON YOUR TEACHING SKILLS - JOURNAL

DAY 23

DATE:-   /   /

1: HOW DISTRACTED DID YOU FIND YOURSELF TODAY WHY WAS THIS? HOW COULD YOU CHANGE THIS FOR THE NEXT LESSON?

2: HOW MOTIVATED WERE YOU TODAY, WHY WAS THIS AND WHAT COULD YOU DO TO IMPROVE THIS?

3: HOW GOOD WERE YOUR COMMUNICATION SKILLS TODAY? WHAT WOULD YOU LIKE TO BE DIFFERENT & HOW CAN YOU START THE CHANGE?

4: WERE YOU PATIENT TODAY? HOW DIFFERENT DO YOU FIND YOURSELF WITH DIFFERENT STUDENTS AND CLASSES? THEN LOOK AT WHY YOU MAY BE DIFFERENT?

REFLECTION ON YOUR TEACHING SKILLS - JOURNAL

 DAY 23

5: WERE YOU ABLE TO DEAL WITH ANY CONFLICT TODAY BOTH STUDENTS AND PEERS? VERY USEFUL TO LOOK AT THIS AREA WITHIN YOURSELF AND WHAT YOU COULD DO DIFFERENTLY.

6: HOW ORGANISED WERE YOU TODAY, TOO MUCH OR TOO LITTLE? WHAT WOULD YOU LIKE TO BE DIFFERENT AND HOW YOU ARE GOING TO DEAL WITH THIS DIFFERENTLY?

7: WERE YOU ENTHUSIASTIC TODAY? HOW DID THE CLASS RESPOND TO YOUR ENTHUSIASM? HOW COULD YOU DEVELOP THIS FURTHER?

8: WERE YOU CONFIDENT TODAY, HOW CONFIDENT ARE YOU ALREADY? COULD THIS BE BETTER WITHIN YOUR STUDENTS AND PEERS.

9: HOW SUPPORTIVE HAVE YOU BEEN TODAY, WHY WAS THIS? WHAT IMPROVEMENTS COULD YOU MAKE TO IMPROVE IN THIS AREA?

REFLECTION ON YOUR TEACHING SKILLS - JOURNAL

DAY 24

DATE:-   /   /

1: HOW DISTRACTED DID YOU FIND YOURSELF TODAY WHY WAS THIS? HOW COULD YOU CHANGE THIS FOR THE NEXT LESSON?

2: HOW MOTIVATED WERE YOU TODAY, WHY WAS THIS AND WHAT COULD YOU DO TO IMPROVE THIS?

3: HOW GOOD WERE YOUR COMMUNICATION SKILLS TODAY? WHAT WOULD YOU LIKE TO BE DIFFERENT & HOW CAN YOU START THE CHANGE?

4: WERE YOU PATIENT TODAY? HOW DIFFERENT DO YOU FIND YOURSELF WITH DIFFERENT STUDENTS AND CLASSES? THEN LOOK AT WHY YOU MAY BE DIFFERENT?

REFLECTION ON YOUR TEACHING SKILLS - JOURNAL

 DAY 24

5: WERE YOU ABLE TO DEAL WITH ANY CONFLICT TODAY BOTH STUDENTS AND PEERS? VERY USEFUL TO LOOK AT THIS AREA WITHIN YOURSELF AND WHAT YOU COULD DO DIFFERENTLY.

6: HOW ORGANISED WERE YOU TODAY, TOO MUCH OR TOO LITTLE? WHAT WOULD YOU LIKE TO BE DIFFERENT AND HOW YOU ARE GOING TO DEAL WITH THIS DIFFERENTLY?

7: WERE YOU ENTHUSIASTIC TODAY? HOW DID THE CLASS RESPOND TO YOUR ENTHUSIASM? HOW COULD YOU DEVELOP THIS FURTHER?

8: WERE YOU CONFIDENT TODAY, HOW CONFIDENT ARE YOU ALREADY? COULD THIS BE BETTER WITHIN YOUR STUDENTS AND PEERS.

9: HOW SUPPORTIVE HAVE YOU BEEN TODAY, WHY WAS THIS? WHAT IMPROVEMENTS COULD YOU MAKE TO IMPROVE IN THIS AREA?

REFLECTION ON YOUR TEACHING SKILLS - JOURNAL

DAY 25

DATE:-   /   /

1: HOW DISTRACTED DID YOU FIND YOURSELF TODAY WHY WAS THIS? HOW COULD YOU CHANGE THIS FOR THE NEXT LESSON?

2: HOW MOTIVATED WERE YOU TODAY, WHY WAS THIS AND WHAT COULD YOU DO TO IMPROVE THIS?

3: HOW GOOD WERE YOUR COMMUNICATION SKILLS TODAY? WHAT WOULD YOU LIKE TO BE DIFFERENT & HOW CAN YOU START THE CHANGE?

4: WERE YOU PATIENT TODAY? HOW DIFFERENT DO YOU FIND YOURSELF WITH DIFFERENT STUDENTS AND CLASSES? THEN LOOK AT WHY YOU MAY BE DIFFERENT?

REFLECTION ON YOUR TEACHING SKILLS - JOURNAL  DAY 25

5: WERE YOU ABLE TO DEAL WITH ANY CONFLICT TODAY BOTH STUDENTS AND PEERS? VERY USEFUL TO LOOK AT THIS AREA WITHIN YOURSELF AND WHAT YOU COULD DO DIFFERENTLY.

6: HOW ORGANISED WERE YOU TODAY, TOO MUCH OR TOO LITTLE? WHAT WOULD YOU LIKE TO BE DIFFERENT AND HOW YOU ARE GOING TO DEAL WITH THIS DIFFERENTLY?

7: WERE YOU ENTHUSIASTIC TODAY? HOW DID THE CLASS RESPOND TO YOUR ENTHUSIASM? HOW COULD YOU DEVELOP THIS FURTHER?

8: WERE YOU CONFIDENT TODAY, HOW CONFIDENT ARE YOU ALREADY? COULD THIS BE BETTER WITHIN YOUR STUDENTS AND PEERS.

9: HOW SUPPORTIVE HAVE YOU BEEN TODAY, WHY WAS THIS? WHAT IMPROVEMENTS COULD YOU MAKE TO IMPROVE IN THIS AREA?

REFLECTION ON YOUR TEACHING SKILLS - JOURNAL

DAY 26

DATE:-   /   /

1: HOW DISTRACTED DID YOU FIND YOURSELF TODAY WHY WAS THIS? HOW COULD YOU CHANGE THIS FOR THE NEXT LESSON?

2: HOW MOTIVATED WERE YOU TODAY, WHY WAS THIS AND WHAT COULD YOU DO TO IMPROVE THIS?

3: HOW GOOD WERE YOUR COMMUNICATION SKILLS TODAY? WHAT WOULD YOU LIKE TO BE DIFFERENT & HOW CAN YOU START THE CHANGE?

4: WERE YOU PATIENT TODAY? HOW DIFFERENT DO YOU FIND YOURSELF WITH DIFFERENT STUDENTS AND CLASSES? THEN LOOK AT WHY YOU MAY BE DIFFERENT?

REFLECTION ON YOUR TEACHING SKILLS - JOURNAL

 DAY 26

5: WERE YOU ABLE TO DEAL WITH ANY CONFLICT TODAY BOTH STUDENTS AND PEERS? VERY USEFUL TO LOOK AT THIS AREA WITHIN YOURSELF AND WHAT YOU COULD DO DIFFERENTLY.

6: HOW ORGANISED WERE YOU TODAY, TOO MUCH OR TOO LITTLE? WHAT WOULD YOU LIKE TO BE DIFFERENT AND HOW YOU ARE GOING TO DEAL WITH THIS DIFFERENTLY?

7: WERE YOU ENTHUSIASTIC TODAY? HOW DID THE CLASS RESPOND TO YOUR ENTHUSIASM? HOW COULD YOU DEVELOP THIS FURTHER?

8: WERE YOU CONFIDENT TODAY, HOW CONFIDENT ARE YOU ALREADY? COULD THIS BE BETTER WITHIN YOUR STUDENTS AND PEERS.

9: HOW SUPPORTIVE HAVE YOU BEEN TODAY, WHY WAS THIS? WHAT IMPROVEMENTS COULD YOU MAKE TO IMPROVE IN THIS AREA?

REFLECTION ON YOUR TEACHING SKILLS - JOURNAL

DAY 27

DATE:-   /   /

1: HOW DISTRACTED DID YOU FIND YOURSELF TODAY WHY WAS THIS? HOW COULD YOU CHANGE THIS FOR THE NEXT LESSON?

2: HOW MOTIVATED WERE YOU TODAY, WHY WAS THIS AND WHAT COULD YOU DO TO IMPROVE THIS?

3: HOW GOOD WERE YOUR COMMUNICATION SKILLS TODAY? WHAT WOULD YOU LIKE TO BE DIFFERENT & HOW CAN YOU START THE CHANGE?

4: WERE YOU PATIENT TODAY? HOW DIFFERENT DO YOU FIND YOURSELF WITH DIFFERENT STUDENTS AND CLASSES? THEN LOOK AT WHY YOU MAY BE DIFFERENT?

REFLECTION ON YOUR TEACHING SKILLS - JOURNAL

 DAY 27

5: WERE YOU ABLE TO DEAL WITH ANY CONFLICT TODAY BOTH STUDENTS AND PEERS? VERY USEFUL TO LOOK AT THIS AREA WITHIN YOURSELF AND WHAT YOU COULD DO DIFFERENTLY.

6: HOW ORGANISED WERE YOU TODAY, TOO MUCH OR TOO LITTLE? WHAT WOULD YOU LIKE TO BE DIFFERENT AND HOW YOU ARE GOING TO DEAL WITH THIS DIFFERENTLY?

7: WERE YOU ENTHUSIASTIC TODAY? HOW DID THE CLASS RESPOND TO YOUR ENTHUSIASM? HOW COULD YOU DEVELOP THIS FURTHER?

8: WERE YOU CONFIDENT TODAY, HOW CONFIDENT ARE YOU ALREADY? COULD THIS BE BETTER WITHIN YOUR STUDENTS AND PEERS.

9: HOW SUPPORTIVE HAVE YOU BEEN TODAY, WHY WAS THIS? WHAT IMPROVEMENTS COULD YOU MAKE TO IMPROVE IN THIS AREA?

REFLECTION ON YOUR TEACHING SKILLS - JOURNAL

DAY 28

DATE:-   /   /

1: HOW DISTRACTED DID YOU FIND YOURSELF TODAY WHY WAS THIS? HOW COULD YOU CHANGE THIS FOR THE NEXT LESSON?

2: HOW MOTIVATED WERE YOU TODAY, WHY WAS THIS AND WHAT COULD YOU DO TO IMPROVE THIS?

3: HOW GOOD WERE YOUR COMMUNICATION SKILLS TODAY? WHAT WOULD YOU LIKE TO BE DIFFERENT & HOW CAN YOU START THE CHANGE?

4: WERE YOU PATIENT TODAY? HOW DIFFERENT DO YOU FIND YOURSELF WITH DIFFERENT STUDENTS AND CLASSES? THEN LOOK AT WHY YOU MAY BE DIFFERENT?

REFLECTION ON YOUR TEACHING SKILLS - JOURNAL

 DAY 28

5: WERE YOU ABLE TO DEAL WITH ANY CONFLICT TODAY BOTH STUDENTS AND PEERS? VERY USEFUL TO LOOK AT THIS AREA WITHIN YOURSELF AND WHAT YOU COULD DO DIFFERENTLY.

6: HOW ORGANISED WERE YOU TODAY, TOO MUCH OR TOO LITTLE? WHAT WOULD YOU LIKE TO BE DIFFERENT AND HOW YOU ARE GOING TO DEAL WITH THIS DIFFERENTLY?

7: WERE YOU ENTHUSIASTIC TODAY? HOW DID THE CLASS RESPOND TO YOUR ENTHUSIASM? HOW COULD YOU DEVELOP THIS FURTHER?

8: WERE YOU CONFIDENT TODAY, HOW CONFIDENT ARE YOU ALREADY? COULD THIS BE BETTER WITHIN YOUR STUDENTS AND PEERS.

9: HOW SUPPORTIVE HAVE YOU BEEN TODAY, WHY WAS THIS? WHAT IMPROVEMENTS COULD YOU MAKE TO IMPROVE IN THIS AREA?

REFLECTION ON YOUR TEACHING SKILLS - JOURNAL

DAY 29

DATE:-   /   /

1: HOW DISTRACTED DID YOU FIND YOURSELF TODAY WHY WAS THIS? HOW COULD YOU CHANGE THIS FOR THE NEXT LESSON?

2: HOW MOTIVATED WERE YOU TODAY, WHY WAS THIS AND WHAT COULD YOU DO TO IMPROVE THIS?

3: HOW GOOD WERE YOUR COMMUNICATION SKILLS TODAY? WHAT WOULD YOU LIKE TO BE DIFFERENT & HOW CAN YOU START THE CHANGE?

4: WERE YOU PATIENT TODAY? HOW DIFFERENT DO YOU FIND YOURSELF WITH DIFFERENT STUDENTS AND CLASSES? THEN LOOK AT WHY YOU MAY BE DIFFERENT?

REFLECTION ON YOUR TEACHING SKILLS - JOURNAL

DAY 29

5: WERE YOU ABLE TO DEAL WITH ANY CONFLICT TODAY BOTH STUDENTS AND PEERS? VERY USEFUL TO LOOK AT THIS AREA WITHIN YOURSELF AND WHAT YOU COULD DO DIFFERENTLY.

6: HOW ORGANISED WERE YOU TODAY, TOO MUCH OR TOO LITTLE? WHAT WOULD YOU LIKE TO BE DIFFERENT AND HOW YOU ARE GOING TO DEAL WITH THIS DIFFERENTLY?

7: WERE YOU ENTHUSIASTIC TODAY? HOW DID THE CLASS RESPOND TO YOUR ENTHUSIASM? HOW COULD YOU DEVELOP THIS FURTHER?

8: WERE YOU CONFIDENT TODAY, HOW CONFIDENT ARE YOU ALREADY? COULD THIS BE BETTER WITHIN YOUR STUDENTS AND PEERS.

9: HOW SUPPORTIVE HAVE YOU BEEN TODAY, WHY WAS THIS? WHAT IMPROVEMENTS COULD YOU MAKE TO IMPROVE IN THIS AREA?

REFLECTION ON YOUR TEACHING SKILLS - JOURNAL

DAY 30

DATE:-   /   /

1: HOW DISTRACTED DID YOU FIND YOURSELF TODAY WHY WAS THIS? HOW COULD YOU CHANGE THIS FOR THE NEXT LESSON?

2: HOW MOTIVATED WERE YOU TODAY, WHY WAS THIS AND WHAT COULD YOU DO TO IMPROVE THIS?

3: HOW GOOD WERE YOUR COMMUNICATION SKILLS TODAY? WHAT WOULD YOU LIKE TO BE DIFFERENT & HOW CAN YOU START THE CHANGE?

4: WERE YOU PATIENT TODAY? HOW DIFFERENT DO YOU FIND YOURSELF WITH DIFFERENT STUDENTS AND CLASSES? THEN LOOK AT WHY YOU MAY BE DIFFERENT?

REFLECTION ON YOUR TEACHING SKILLS - JOURNAL

 DAY 30

> **5: WERE YOU ABLE TO DEAL WITH ANY CONFLICT TODAY BOTH STUDENTS AND PEERS? VERY USEFUL TO LOOK AT THIS AREA WITHIN YOURSELF AND WHAT YOU COULD DO DIFFERENTLY.**

> **6: HOW ORGANISED WERE YOU TODAY, TOO MUCH OR TOO LITTLE? WHAT WOULD YOU LIKE TO BE DIFFERENT AND HOW YOU ARE GOING TO DEAL WITH THIS DIFFERENTLY?**

> **7: WERE YOU ENTHUSIASTIC TODAY? HOW DID THE CLASS RESPOND TO YOUR ENTHUSIASM? HOW COULD YOU DEVELOP THIS FURTHER?**

> **8: WERE YOU CONFIDENT TODAY, HOW CONFIDENT ARE YOU ALREADY? COULD THIS BE BETTER WITHIN YOUR STUDENTS AND PEERS.**

> **9: HOW SUPPORTIVE HAVE YOU BEEN TODAY, WHY WAS THIS? WHAT IMPROVEMENTS COULD YOU MAKE TO IMPROVE IN THIS AREA?**

REFLECTION ON YOUR TEACHING SKILLS - JOURNAL

DAY 21 - 30 REVIEW

1: HOW HAVE I GROWN OVER THE LAST 10 DAYS?

2: WHAT AM I GOING TO FOCUS ON OVER THE NEXT 10 DAYS?

3: WHAT FIVE THINGS AM I POSITIVELY TAKING FROM THE LAST 10 DAYS AND MOVING THEM FORWARD INTO THE NEXT 10 DAYS.

-
-
-
-
-

4: WHAT KEY AREAS WOULD I LIKE TO CONCENTRATE ON TO IMPROVE MY TEACHING SKILLS FURTHER?

"One good teacher in a lifetime may sometimes change a delinquent into a solid citizen."

REFLECTION ON YOUR TEACHING SKILLS - JOURNAL

DAY 31

DATE:-   /   /

1: HOW DISTRACTED DID YOU FIND YOURSELF TODAY WHY WAS THIS? HOW COULD YOU CHANGE THIS FOR THE NEXT LESSON?

2: HOW MOTIVATED WERE YOU TODAY, WHY WAS THIS AND WHAT COULD YOU DO TO IMPROVE THIS?

3: HOW GOOD WERE YOUR COMMUNICATION SKILLS TODAY? WHAT WOULD YOU LIKE TO BE DIFFERENT & HOW CAN YOU START THE CHANGE?

4: WERE YOU PATIENT TODAY? HOW DIFFERENT DO YOU FIND YOURSELF WITH DIFFERENT STUDENTS AND CLASSES? THEN LOOK AT WHY YOU MAY BE DIFFERENT?

REFLECTION ON YOUR TEACHING SKILLS - JOURNAL

 DAY 31

5: WERE YOU ABLE TO DEAL WITH ANY CONFLICT TODAY BOTH STUDENTS AND PEERS? VERY USEFUL TO LOOK AT THIS AREA WITHIN YOURSELF AND WHAT YOU COULD DO DIFFERENTLY.

6: HOW ORGANISED WERE YOU TODAY, TOO MUCH OR TOO LITTLE? WHAT WOULD YOU LIKE TO BE DIFFERENT AND HOW YOU ARE GOING TO DEAL WITH THIS DIFFERENTLY?

7: WERE YOU ENTHUSIASTIC TODAY? HOW DID THE CLASS RESPOND TO YOUR ENTHUSIASM? HOW COULD YOU DEVELOP THIS FURTHER?

8: WERE YOU CONFIDENT TODAY, HOW CONFIDENT ARE YOU ALREADY? COULD THIS BE BETTER WITHIN YOUR STUDENTS AND PEERS.

9: HOW SUPPORTIVE HAVE YOU BEEN TODAY, WHY WAS THIS? WHAT IMPROVEMENTS COULD YOU MAKE TO IMPROVE IN THIS AREA?

REFLECTION ON YOUR TEACHING SKILLS - JOURNAL

DAY 32

DATE:-   /   /

1: HOW DISTRACTED DID YOU FIND YOURSELF TODAY WHY WAS THIS? HOW COULD YOU CHANGE THIS FOR THE NEXT LESSON?

2: HOW MOTIVATED WERE YOU TODAY, WHY WAS THIS AND WHAT COULD YOU DO TO IMPROVE THIS?

3: HOW GOOD WERE YOUR COMMUNICATION SKILLS TODAY? WHAT WOULD YOU LIKE TO BE DIFFERENT & HOW CAN YOU START THE CHANGE?

4: WERE YOU PATIENT TODAY? HOW DIFFERENT DO YOU FIND YOURSELF WITH DIFFERENT STUDENTS AND CLASSES? THEN LOOK AT WHY YOU MAY BE DIFFERENT?

REFLECTION ON YOUR TEACHING SKILLS - JOURNAL

 DAY 32

5: WERE YOU ABLE TO DEAL WITH ANY CONFLICT TODAY BOTH STUDENTS AND PEERS? VERY USEFUL TO LOOK AT THIS AREA WITHIN YOURSELF AND WHAT YOU COULD DO DIFFERENTLY.

6: HOW ORGANISED WERE YOU TODAY, TOO MUCH OR TOO LITTLE? WHAT WOULD YOU LIKE TO BE DIFFERENT AND HOW YOU ARE GOING TO DEAL WITH THIS DIFFERENTLY?

7: WERE YOU ENTHUSIASTIC TODAY? HOW DID THE CLASS RESPOND TO YOUR ENTHUSIASM? HOW COULD YOU DEVELOP THIS FURTHER?

8: WERE YOU CONFIDENT TODAY, HOW CONFIDENT ARE YOU ALREADY? COULD THIS BE BETTER WITHIN YOUR STUDENTS AND PEERS.

9: HOW SUPPORTIVE HAVE YOU BEEN TODAY, WHY WAS THIS? WHAT IMPROVEMENTS COULD YOU MAKE TO IMPROVE IN THIS AREA?

REFLECTION ON YOUR TEACHING SKILLS - JOURNAL

DAY 33

DATE:-   /   /

1: HOW DISTRACTED DID YOU FIND YOURSELF TODAY WHY WAS THIS? HOW COULD YOU CHANGE THIS FOR THE NEXT LESSON?

2: HOW MOTIVATED WERE YOU TODAY, WHY WAS THIS AND WHAT COULD YOU DO TO IMPROVE THIS?

3: HOW GOOD WERE YOUR COMMUNICATION SKILLS TODAY? WHAT WOULD YOU LIKE TO BE DIFFERENT & HOW CAN YOU START THE CHANGE?

4: WERE YOU PATIENT TODAY? HOW DIFFERENT DO YOU FIND YOURSELF WITH DIFFERENT STUDENTS AND CLASSES? THEN LOOK AT WHY YOU MAY BE DIFFERENT?

REFLECTION ON YOUR TEACHING SKILLS - JOURNAL

 DAY 33

5: WERE YOU ABLE TO DEAL WITH ANY CONFLICT TODAY BOTH STUDENTS AND PEERS? VERY USEFUL TO LOOK AT THIS AREA WITHIN YOURSELF AND WHAT YOU COULD DO DIFFERENTLY.

6: HOW ORGANISED WERE YOU TODAY, TOO MUCH OR TOO LITTLE? WHAT WOULD YOU LIKE TO BE DIFFERENT AND HOW YOU ARE GOING TO DEAL WITH THIS DIFFERENTLY?

7: WERE YOU ENTHUSIASTIC TODAY? HOW DID THE CLASS RESPOND TO YOUR ENTHUSIASM? HOW COULD YOU DEVELOP THIS FURTHER?

8: WERE YOU CONFIDENT TODAY, HOW CONFIDENT ARE YOU ALREADY? COULD THIS BE BETTER WITHIN YOUR STUDENTS AND PEERS.

9: HOW SUPPORTIVE HAVE YOU BEEN TODAY, WHY WAS THIS? WHAT IMPROVEMENTS COULD YOU MAKE TO IMPROVE IN THIS AREA?

REFLECTION ON YOUR TEACHING SKILLS - JOURNAL

DAY 34

DATE:-   /   /

1: HOW DISTRACTED DID YOU FIND YOURSELF TODAY WHY WAS THIS? HOW COULD YOU CHANGE THIS FOR THE NEXT LESSON?

2: HOW MOTIVATED WERE YOU TODAY, WHY WAS THIS AND WHAT COULD YOU DO TO IMPROVE THIS?

3: HOW GOOD WERE YOUR COMMUNICATION SKILLS TODAY? WHAT WOULD YOU LIKE TO BE DIFFERENT & HOW CAN YOU START THE CHANGE?

4: WERE YOU PATIENT TODAY? HOW DIFFERENT DO YOU FIND YOURSELF WITH DIFFERENT STUDENTS AND CLASSES? THEN LOOK AT WHY YOU MAY BE DIFFERENT?

REFLECTION ON YOUR TEACHING SKILLS - JOURNAL

 DAY 34

5: WERE YOU ABLE TO DEAL WITH ANY CONFLICT TODAY BOTH STUDENTS AND PEERS? VERY USEFUL TO LOOK AT THIS AREA WITHIN YOURSELF AND WHAT YOU COULD DO DIFFERENTLY.

6: HOW ORGANISED WERE YOU TODAY, TOO MUCH OR TOO LITTLE? WHAT WOULD YOU LIKE TO BE DIFFERENT AND HOW YOU ARE GOING TO DEAL WITH THIS DIFFERENTLY?

7: WERE YOU ENTHUSIASTIC TODAY? HOW DID THE CLASS RESPOND TO YOUR ENTHUSIASM? HOW COULD YOU DEVELOP THIS FURTHER?

8: WERE YOU CONFIDENT TODAY, HOW CONFIDENT ARE YOU ALREADY? COULD THIS BE BETTER WITHIN YOUR STUDENTS AND PEERS.

9: HOW SUPPORTIVE HAVE YOU BEEN TODAY, WHY WAS THIS? WHAT IMPROVEMENTS COULD YOU MAKE TO IMPROVE IN THIS AREA?

REFLECTION ON YOUR TEACHING SKILLS - JOURNAL

DAY 35

DATE:-   /   /

1: HOW DISTRACTED DID YOU FIND YOURSELF TODAY WHY WAS THIS? HOW COULD YOU CHANGE THIS FOR THE NEXT LESSON?

2: HOW MOTIVATED WERE YOU TODAY, WHY WAS THIS AND WHAT COULD YOU DO TO IMPROVE THIS?

3: HOW GOOD WERE YOUR COMMUNICATION SKILLS TODAY? WHAT WOULD YOU LIKE TO BE DIFFERENT & HOW CAN YOU START THE CHANGE?

4: WERE YOU PATIENT TODAY? HOW DIFFERENT DO YOU FIND YOURSELF WITH DIFFERENT STUDENTS AND CLASSES? THEN LOOK AT WHY YOU MAY BE DIFFERENT?

REFLECTION ON YOUR TEACHING SKILLS - JOURNAL

 DAY 35

5: WERE YOU ABLE TO DEAL WITH ANY CONFLICT TODAY BOTH STUDENTS AND PEERS? VERY USEFUL TO LOOK AT THIS AREA WITHIN YOURSELF AND WHAT YOU COULD DO DIFFERENTLY.

6: HOW ORGANISED WERE YOU TODAY, TOO MUCH OR TOO LITTLE? WHAT WOULD YOU LIKE TO BE DIFFERENT AND HOW YOU ARE GOING TO DEAL WITH THIS DIFFERENTLY?

7: WERE YOU ENTHUSIASTIC TODAY? HOW DID THE CLASS RESPOND TO YOUR ENTHUSIASM? HOW COULD YOU DEVELOP THIS FURTHER?

8: WERE YOU CONFIDENT TODAY, HOW CONFIDENT ARE YOU ALREADY? COULD THIS BE BETTER WITHIN YOUR STUDENTS AND PEERS.

9: HOW SUPPORTIVE HAVE YOU BEEN TODAY, WHY WAS THIS? WHAT IMPROVEMENTS COULD YOU MAKE TO IMPROVE IN THIS AREA?

REFLECTION ON YOUR TEACHING SKILLS - JOURNAL

DAY 36

DATE:-   /   /

1: HOW DISTRACTED DID YOU FIND YOURSELF TODAY WHY WAS THIS? HOW COULD YOU CHANGE THIS FOR THE NEXT LESSON?

2: HOW MOTIVATED WERE YOU TODAY, WHY WAS THIS AND WHAT COULD YOU DO TO IMPROVE THIS?

3: HOW GOOD WERE YOUR COMMUNICATION SKILLS TODAY? WHAT WOULD YOU LIKE TO BE DIFFERENT & HOW CAN YOU START THE CHANGE?

4: WERE YOU PATIENT TODAY? HOW DIFFERENT DO YOU FIND YOURSELF WITH DIFFERENT STUDENTS AND CLASSES? THEN LOOK AT WHY YOU MAY BE DIFFERENT?

REFLECTION ON YOUR TEACHING SKILLS - JOURNAL

 DAY 36

5: WERE YOU ABLE TO DEAL WITH ANY CONFLICT TODAY BOTH STUDENTS AND PEERS? VERY USEFUL TO LOOK AT THIS AREA WITHIN YOURSELF AND WHAT YOU COULD DO DIFFERENTLY.

6: HOW ORGANISED WERE YOU TODAY, TOO MUCH OR TOO LITTLE? WHAT WOULD YOU LIKE TO BE DIFFERENT AND HOW YOU ARE GOING TO DEAL WITH THIS DIFFERENTLY?

7: WERE YOU ENTHUSIASTIC TODAY? HOW DID THE CLASS RESPOND TO YOUR ENTHUSIASM? HOW COULD YOU DEVELOP THIS FURTHER?

8: WERE YOU CONFIDENT TODAY, HOW CONFIDENT ARE YOU ALREADY? COULD THIS BE BETTER WITHIN YOUR STUDENTS AND PEERS.

9: HOW SUPPORTIVE HAVE YOU BEEN TODAY, WHY WAS THIS? WHAT IMPROVEMENTS COULD YOU MAKE TO IMPROVE IN THIS AREA?

REFLECTION ON YOUR TEACHING SKILLS - JOURNAL

DAY 37

DATE:-   /   /

1: HOW DISTRACTED DID YOU FIND YOURSELF TODAY WHY WAS THIS? HOW COULD YOU CHANGE THIS FOR THE NEXT LESSON?

2: HOW MOTIVATED WERE YOU TODAY, WHY WAS THIS AND WHAT COULD YOU DO TO IMPROVE THIS?

3: HOW GOOD WERE YOUR COMMUNICATION SKILLS TODAY? WHAT WOULD YOU LIKE TO BE DIFFERENT & HOW CAN YOU START THE CHANGE?

4: WERE YOU PATIENT TODAY? HOW DIFFERENT DO YOU FIND YOURSELF WITH DIFFERENT STUDENTS AND CLASSES? THEN LOOK AT WHY YOU MAY BE DIFFERENT?

REFLECTION ON YOUR TEACHING SKILLS - JOURNAL  DAY 37

5: WERE YOU ABLE TO DEAL WITH ANY CONFLICT TODAY BOTH STUDENTS AND PEERS? VERY USEFUL TO LOOK AT THIS AREA WITHIN YOURSELF AND WHAT YOU COULD DO DIFFERENTLY.

6: HOW ORGANISED WERE YOU TODAY, TOO MUCH OR TOO LITTLE? WHAT WOULD YOU LIKE TO BE DIFFERENT AND HOW YOU ARE GOING TO DEAL WITH THIS DIFFERENTLY?

7: WERE YOU ENTHUSIASTIC TODAY? HOW DID THE CLASS RESPOND TO YOUR ENTHUSIASM? HOW COULD YOU DEVELOP THIS FURTHER?

8: WERE YOU CONFIDENT TODAY, HOW CONFIDENT ARE YOU ALREADY? COULD THIS BE BETTER WITHIN YOUR STUDENTS AND PEERS.

9: HOW SUPPORTIVE HAVE YOU BEEN TODAY, WHY WAS THIS? WHAT IMPROVEMENTS COULD YOU MAKE TO IMPROVE IN THIS AREA?

REFLECTION ON YOUR TEACHING SKILLS - JOURNAL

DAY 38

DATE:-   /   /

1: HOW DISTRACTED DID YOU FIND YOURSELF TODAY WHY WAS THIS? HOW COULD YOU CHANGE THIS FOR THE NEXT LESSON?

2: HOW MOTIVATED WERE YOU TODAY, WHY WAS THIS AND WHAT COULD YOU DO TO IMPROVE THIS?

3: HOW GOOD WERE YOUR COMMUNICATION SKILLS TODAY? WHAT WOULD YOU LIKE TO BE DIFFERENT & HOW CAN YOU START THE CHANGE?

4: WERE YOU PATIENT TODAY? HOW DIFFERENT DO YOU FIND YOURSELF WITH DIFFERENT STUDENTS AND CLASSES? THEN LOOK AT WHY YOU MAY BE DIFFERENT?

REFLECTION ON YOUR TEACHING SKILLS - JOURNAL

 DAY 38

5: WERE YOU ABLE TO DEAL WITH ANY CONFLICT TODAY BOTH STUDENTS AND PEERS? VERY USEFUL TO LOOK AT THIS AREA WITHIN YOURSELF AND WHAT YOU COULD DO DIFFERENTLY.

6: HOW ORGANISED WERE YOU TODAY, TOO MUCH OR TOO LITTLE? WHAT WOULD YOU LIKE TO BE DIFFERENT AND HOW YOU ARE GOING TO DEAL WITH THIS DIFFERENTLY?

7: WERE YOU ENTHUSIASTIC TODAY? HOW DID THE CLASS RESPOND TO YOUR ENTHUSIASM? HOW COULD YOU DEVELOP THIS FURTHER?

8: WERE YOU CONFIDENT TODAY, HOW CONFIDENT ARE YOU ALREADY? COULD THIS BE BETTER WITHIN YOUR STUDENTS AND PEERS.

9: HOW SUPPORTIVE HAVE YOU BEEN TODAY, WHY WAS THIS? WHAT IMPROVEMENTS COULD YOU MAKE TO IMPROVE IN THIS AREA?

REFLECTION ON YOUR TEACHING SKILLS - JOURNAL

DAY 39

DATE:-   /   /

1: HOW DISTRACTED DID YOU FIND YOURSELF TODAY WHY WAS THIS? HOW COULD YOU CHANGE THIS FOR THE NEXT LESSON?

2: HOW MOTIVATED WERE YOU TODAY, WHY WAS THIS AND WHAT COULD YOU DO TO IMPROVE THIS?

3: HOW GOOD WERE YOUR COMMUNICATION SKILLS TODAY? WHAT WOULD YOU LIKE TO BE DIFFERENT & HOW CAN YOU START THE CHANGE?

4: WERE YOU PATIENT TODAY? HOW DIFFERENT DO YOU FIND YOURSELF WITH DIFFERENT STUDENTS AND CLASSES? THEN LOOK AT WHY YOU MAY BE DIFFERENT?

REFLECTION ON YOUR TEACHING SKILLS - JOURNAL

 DAY 39

5: WERE YOU ABLE TO DEAL WITH ANY CONFLICT TODAY BOTH STUDENTS AND PEERS? VERY USEFUL TO LOOK AT THIS AREA WITHIN YOURSELF AND WHAT YOU COULD DO DIFFERENTLY.

6: HOW ORGANISED WERE YOU TODAY, TOO MUCH OR TOO LITTLE? WHAT WOULD YOU LIKE TO BE DIFFERENT AND HOW YOU ARE GOING TO DEAL WITH THIS DIFFERENTLY?

7: WERE YOU ENTHUSIASTIC TODAY? HOW DID THE CLASS RESPOND TO YOUR ENTHUSIASM? HOW COULD YOU DEVELOP THIS FURTHER?

8: WERE YOU CONFIDENT TODAY, HOW CONFIDENT ARE YOU ALREADY? COULD THIS BE BETTER WITHIN YOUR STUDENTS AND PEERS.

9: HOW SUPPORTIVE HAVE YOU BEEN TODAY, WHY WAS THIS? WHAT IMPROVEMENTS COULD YOU MAKE TO IMPROVE IN THIS AREA?

REFLECTION ON YOUR TEACHING SKILLS - JOURNAL

DAY 40

DATE:-   /   /

1: HOW DISTRACTED DID YOU FIND YOURSELF TODAY WHY WAS THIS? HOW COULD YOU CHANGE THIS FOR THE NEXT LESSON?

2: HOW MOTIVATED WERE YOU TODAY, WHY WAS THIS AND WHAT COULD YOU DO TO IMPROVE THIS?

3: HOW GOOD WERE YOUR COMMUNICATION SKILLS TODAY? WHAT WOULD YOU LIKE TO BE DIFFERENT & HOW CAN YOU START THE CHANGE?

4: WERE YOU PATIENT TODAY? HOW DIFFERENT DO YOU FIND YOURSELF WITH DIFFERENT STUDENTS AND CLASSES? THEN LOOK AT WHY YOU MAY BE DIFFERENT?

REFLECTION ON YOUR TEACHING SKILLS - JOURNAL

 DAY 40

5: WERE YOU ABLE TO DEAL WITH ANY CONFLICT TODAY BOTH STUDENTS AND PEERS? VERY USEFUL TO LOOK AT THIS AREA WITHIN YOURSELF AND WHAT YOU COULD DO DIFFERENTLY.

6: HOW ORGANISED WERE YOU TODAY, TOO MUCH OR TOO LITTLE? WHAT WOULD YOU LIKE TO BE DIFFERENT AND HOW YOU ARE GOING TO DEAL WITH THIS DIFFERENTLY?

7: WERE YOU ENTHUSIASTIC TODAY? HOW DID THE CLASS RESPOND TO YOUR ENTHUSIASM? HOW COULD YOU DEVELOP THIS FURTHER?

8: WERE YOU CONFIDENT TODAY, HOW CONFIDENT ARE YOU ALREADY? COULD THIS BE BETTER WITHIN YOUR STUDENTS AND PEERS.

9: HOW SUPPORTIVE HAVE YOU BEEN TODAY, WHY WAS THIS? WHAT IMPROVEMENTS COULD YOU MAKE TO IMPROVE IN THIS AREA?

REFLECTION ON YOUR TEACHING SKILLS - JOURNAL

DAY 31 - 40 REVIEW

1: HOW HAVE I GROWN OVER THE LAST 10 DAYS?

2: WHAT AM I GOING TO FOCUS ON OVER THE NEXT 10 DAYS?

3: WHAT FIVE THINGS AM I POSITIVELY TAKING FROM THE LAST 10 DAYS AND MOVING THEM FORWARD INTO THE NEXT 10 DAYS.

-
-
-
-
-

4: WHAT KEY AREAS WOULD I LIKE TO CONCENTRATE ON TO IMPROVE MY TEACHING SKILLS FURTHER?

> "So, a good teacher always makes you do something a little bit more than you thought that you could do."

REFLECTION ON YOUR TEACHING SKILLS - JOURNAL

DAY 41

DATE:-   /   /

1: HOW DISTRACTED DID YOU FIND YOURSELF TODAY WHY WAS THIS? HOW COULD YOU CHANGE THIS FOR THE NEXT LESSON?

2: HOW MOTIVATED WERE YOU TODAY, WHY WAS THIS AND WHAT COULD YOU DO TO IMPROVE THIS?

3: HOW GOOD WERE YOUR COMMUNICATION SKILLS TODAY? WHAT WOULD YOU LIKE TO BE DIFFERENT & HOW CAN YOU START THE CHANGE?

4: WERE YOU PATIENT TODAY? HOW DIFFERENT DO YOU FIND YOURSELF WITH DIFFERENT STUDENTS AND CLASSES? THEN LOOK AT WHY YOU MAY BE DIFFERENT?

REFLECTION ON YOUR TEACHING SKILLS - JOURNAL  DAY 41

5: WERE YOU ABLE TO DEAL WITH ANY CONFLICT TODAY BOTH STUDENTS AND PEERS? VERY USEFUL TO LOOK AT THIS AREA WITHIN YOURSELF AND WHAT YOU COULD DO DIFFERENTLY.

6: HOW ORGANISED WERE YOU TODAY, TOO MUCH OR TOO LITTLE? WHAT WOULD YOU LIKE TO BE DIFFERENT AND HOW YOU ARE GOING TO DEAL WITH THIS DIFFERENTLY?

7: WERE YOU ENTHUSIASTIC TODAY? HOW DID THE CLASS RESPOND TO YOUR ENTHUSIASM? HOW COULD YOU DEVELOP THIS FURTHER?

8: WERE YOU CONFIDENT TODAY, HOW CONFIDENT ARE YOU ALREADY? COULD THIS BE BETTER WITHIN YOUR STUDENTS AND PEERS.

9: HOW SUPPORTIVE HAVE YOU BEEN TODAY, WHY WAS THIS? WHAT IMPROVEMENTS COULD YOU MAKE TO IMPROVE IN THIS AREA?

REFLECTION ON YOUR TEACHING SKILLS - JOURNAL

DAY 42

DATE:-   /   /

1: HOW DISTRACTED DID YOU FIND YOURSELF TODAY WHY WAS THIS? HOW COULD YOU CHANGE THIS FOR THE NEXT LESSON?

2: HOW MOTIVATED WERE YOU TODAY, WHY WAS THIS AND WHAT COULD YOU DO TO IMPROVE THIS?

3: HOW GOOD WERE YOUR COMMUNICATION SKILLS TODAY? WHAT WOULD YOU LIKE TO BE DIFFERENT & HOW CAN YOU START THE CHANGE?

4: WERE YOU PATIENT TODAY? HOW DIFFERENT DO YOU FIND YOURSELF WITH DIFFERENT STUDENTS AND CLASSES? THEN LOOK AT WHY YOU MAY BE DIFFERENT?

REFLECTION ON YOUR TEACHING SKILLS - JOURNAL

 DAY 42

5: WERE YOU ABLE TO DEAL WITH ANY CONFLICT TODAY BOTH STUDENTS AND PEERS? VERY USEFUL TO LOOK AT THIS AREA WITHIN YOURSELF AND WHAT YOU COULD DO DIFFERENTLY.

6: HOW ORGANISED WERE YOU TODAY, TOO MUCH OR TOO LITTLE? WHAT WOULD YOU LIKE TO BE DIFFERENT AND HOW YOU ARE GOING TO DEAL WITH THIS DIFFERENTLY?

7: WERE YOU ENTHUSIASTIC TODAY? HOW DID THE CLASS RESPOND TO YOUR ENTHUSIASM? HOW COULD YOU DEVELOP THIS FURTHER?

8: WERE YOU CONFIDENT TODAY, HOW CONFIDENT ARE YOU ALREADY? COULD THIS BE BETTER WITHIN YOUR STUDENTS AND PEERS.

9: HOW SUPPORTIVE HAVE YOU BEEN TODAY, WHY WAS THIS? WHAT IMPROVEMENTS COULD YOU MAKE TO IMPROVE IN THIS AREA?

REFLECTION ON YOUR TEACHING SKILLS - JOURNAL

DAY 43

DATE:-   /   /

1: HOW DISTRACTED DID YOU FIND YOURSELF TODAY WHY WAS THIS? HOW COULD YOU CHANGE THIS FOR THE NEXT LESSON?

2: HOW MOTIVATED WERE YOU TODAY, WHY WAS THIS AND WHAT COULD YOU DO TO IMPROVE THIS?

3: HOW GOOD WERE YOUR COMMUNICATION SKILLS TODAY? WHAT WOULD YOU LIKE TO BE DIFFERENT & HOW CAN YOU START THE CHANGE?

4: WERE YOU PATIENT TODAY? HOW DIFFERENT DO YOU FIND YOURSELF WITH DIFFERENT STUDENTS AND CLASSES? THEN LOOK AT WHY YOU MAY BE DIFFERENT?

REFLECTION ON YOUR TEACHING SKILLS - JOURNAL

 DAY 43

5: WERE YOU ABLE TO DEAL WITH ANY CONFLICT TODAY BOTH STUDENTS AND PEERS? VERY USEFUL TO LOOK AT THIS AREA WITHIN YOURSELF AND WHAT YOU COULD DO DIFFERENTLY.

6: HOW ORGANISED WERE YOU TODAY, TOO MUCH OR TOO LITTLE? WHAT WOULD YOU LIKE TO BE DIFFERENT AND HOW YOU ARE GOING TO DEAL WITH THIS DIFFERENTLY?

7: WERE YOU ENTHUSIASTIC TODAY? HOW DID THE CLASS RESPOND TO YOUR ENTHUSIASM? HOW COULD YOU DEVELOP THIS FURTHER?

8: WERE YOU CONFIDENT TODAY, HOW CONFIDENT ARE YOU ALREADY? COULD THIS BE BETTER WITHIN YOUR STUDENTS AND PEERS.

9: HOW SUPPORTIVE HAVE YOU BEEN TODAY, WHY WAS THIS? WHAT IMPROVEMENTS COULD YOU MAKE TO IMPROVE IN THIS AREA?

REFLECTION ON YOUR TEACHING SKILLS - JOURNAL

DAY 44

DATE:-   /   /

1: HOW DISTRACTED DID YOU FIND YOURSELF TODAY WHY WAS THIS? HOW COULD YOU CHANGE THIS FOR THE NEXT LESSON?

2: HOW MOTIVATED WERE YOU TODAY, WHY WAS THIS AND WHAT COULD YOU DO TO IMPROVE THIS?

3: HOW GOOD WERE YOUR COMMUNICATION SKILLS TODAY? WHAT WOULD YOU LIKE TO BE DIFFERENT & HOW CAN YOU START THE CHANGE?

4: WERE YOU PATIENT TODAY? HOW DIFFERENT DO YOU FIND YOURSELF WITH DIFFERENT STUDENTS AND CLASSES? THEN LOOK AT WHY YOU MAY BE DIFFERENT?

REFLECTION ON YOUR TEACHING SKILLS - JOURNAL

 DAY 44

5: WERE YOU ABLE TO DEAL WITH ANY CONFLICT TODAY BOTH STUDENTS AND PEERS? VERY USEFUL TO LOOK AT THIS AREA WITHIN YOURSELF AND WHAT YOU COULD DO DIFFERENTLY.

6: HOW ORGANISED WERE YOU TODAY, TOO MUCH OR TOO LITTLE? WHAT WOULD YOU LIKE TO BE DIFFERENT AND HOW YOU ARE GOING TO DEAL WITH THIS DIFFERENTLY?

7: WERE YOU ENTHUSIASTIC TODAY? HOW DID THE CLASS RESPOND TO YOUR ENTHUSIASM? HOW COULD YOU DEVELOP THIS FURTHER?

8: WERE YOU CONFIDENT TODAY, HOW CONFIDENT ARE YOU ALREADY? COULD THIS BE BETTER WITHIN YOUR STUDENTS AND PEERS.

9: HOW SUPPORTIVE HAVE YOU BEEN TODAY, WHY WAS THIS? WHAT IMPROVEMENTS COULD YOU MAKE TO IMPROVE IN THIS AREA?

REFLECTION ON YOUR TEACHING SKILLS - JOURNAL

DAY 45

DATE:-   /   /

1: HOW DISTRACTED DID YOU FIND YOURSELF TODAY WHY WAS THIS? HOW COULD YOU CHANGE THIS FOR THE NEXT LESSON?

2: HOW MOTIVATED WERE YOU TODAY, WHY WAS THIS AND WHAT COULD YOU DO TO IMPROVE THIS?

3: HOW GOOD WERE YOUR COMMUNICATION SKILLS TODAY? WHAT WOULD YOU LIKE TO BE DIFFERENT & HOW CAN YOU START THE CHANGE?

4: WERE YOU PATIENT TODAY? HOW DIFFERENT DO YOU FIND YOURSELF WITH DIFFERENT STUDENTS AND CLASSES? THEN LOOK AT WHY YOU MAY BE DIFFERENT?

REFLECTION ON YOUR TEACHING SKILLS - JOURNAL

 DAY 45

5: WERE YOU ABLE TO DEAL WITH ANY CONFLICT TODAY BOTH STUDENTS AND PEERS? VERY USEFUL TO LOOK AT THIS AREA WITHIN YOURSELF AND WHAT YOU COULD DO DIFFERENTLY.

6: HOW ORGANISED WERE YOU TODAY, TOO MUCH OR TOO LITTLE? WHAT WOULD YOU LIKE TO BE DIFFERENT AND HOW YOU ARE GOING TO DEAL WITH THIS DIFFERENTLY?

7: WERE YOU ENTHUSIASTIC TODAY? HOW DID THE CLASS RESPOND TO YOUR ENTHUSIASM? HOW COULD YOU DEVELOP THIS FURTHER?

8: WERE YOU CONFIDENT TODAY, HOW CONFIDENT ARE YOU ALREADY? COULD THIS BE BETTER WITHIN YOUR STUDENTS AND PEERS.

9: HOW SUPPORTIVE HAVE YOU BEEN TODAY, WHY WAS THIS? WHAT IMPROVEMENTS COULD YOU MAKE TO IMPROVE IN THIS AREA?

REFLECTION ON YOUR TEACHING SKILLS - JOURNAL

DAY 46

DATE:-   /   /

1: HOW DISTRACTED DID YOU FIND YOURSELF TODAY WHY WAS THIS? HOW COULD YOU CHANGE THIS FOR THE NEXT LESSON?

2: HOW MOTIVATED WERE YOU TODAY, WHY WAS THIS AND WHAT COULD YOU DO TO IMPROVE THIS?

3: HOW GOOD WERE YOUR COMMUNICATION SKILLS TODAY? WHAT WOULD YOU LIKE TO BE DIFFERENT & HOW CAN YOU START THE CHANGE?

4: WERE YOU PATIENT TODAY? HOW DIFFERENT DO YOU FIND YOURSELF WITH DIFFERENT STUDENTS AND CLASSES? THEN LOOK AT WHY YOU MAY BE DIFFERENT?

REFLECTION ON YOUR TEACHING SKILLS - JOURNAL

 DAY 46

5: WERE YOU ABLE TO DEAL WITH ANY CONFLICT TODAY BOTH STUDENTS AND PEERS? VERY USEFUL TO LOOK AT THIS AREA WITHIN YOURSELF AND WHAT YOU COULD DO DIFFERENTLY.

6: HOW ORGANISED WERE YOU TODAY, TOO MUCH OR TOO LITTLE? WHAT WOULD YOU LIKE TO BE DIFFERENT AND HOW YOU ARE GOING TO DEAL WITH THIS DIFFERENTLY?

7: WERE YOU ENTHUSIASTIC TODAY? HOW DID THE CLASS RESPOND TO YOUR ENTHUSIASM? HOW COULD YOU DEVELOP THIS FURTHER?

8: WERE YOU CONFIDENT TODAY, HOW CONFIDENT ARE YOU ALREADY? COULD THIS BE BETTER WITHIN YOUR STUDENTS AND PEERS.

9: HOW SUPPORTIVE HAVE YOU BEEN TODAY, WHY WAS THIS? WHAT IMPROVEMENTS COULD YOU MAKE TO IMPROVE IN THIS AREA?

REFLECTION ON YOUR TEACHING SKILLS - JOURNAL

DAY 47

DATE:-   /   /

1: HOW DISTRACTED DID YOU FIND YOURSELF TODAY WHY WAS THIS? HOW COULD YOU CHANGE THIS FOR THE NEXT LESSON?

2: HOW MOTIVATED WERE YOU TODAY, WHY WAS THIS AND WHAT COULD YOU DO TO IMPROVE THIS?

3: HOW GOOD WERE YOUR COMMUNICATION SKILLS TODAY? WHAT WOULD YOU LIKE TO BE DIFFERENT & HOW CAN YOU START THE CHANGE?

4: WERE YOU PATIENT TODAY? HOW DIFFERENT DO YOU FIND YOURSELF WITH DIFFERENT STUDENTS AND CLASSES? THEN LOOK AT WHY YOU MAY BE DIFFERENT?

REFLECTION ON YOUR TEACHING SKILLS - JOURNAL

 DAY 47

5: WERE YOU ABLE TO DEAL WITH ANY CONFLICT TODAY BOTH STUDENTS AND PEERS? VERY USEFUL TO LOOK AT THIS AREA WITHIN YOURSELF AND WHAT YOU COULD DO DIFFERENTLY.

6: HOW ORGANISED WERE YOU TODAY, TOO MUCH OR TOO LITTLE? WHAT WOULD YOU LIKE TO BE DIFFERENT AND HOW YOU ARE GOING TO DEAL WITH THIS DIFFERENTLY?

7: WERE YOU ENTHUSIASTIC TODAY? HOW DID THE CLASS RESPOND TO YOUR ENTHUSIASM? HOW COULD YOU DEVELOP THIS FURTHER?

8: WERE YOU CONFIDENT TODAY, HOW CONFIDENT ARE YOU ALREADY? COULD THIS BE BETTER WITHIN YOUR STUDENTS AND PEERS.

9: HOW SUPPORTIVE HAVE YOU BEEN TODAY, WHY WAS THIS? WHAT IMPROVEMENTS COULD YOU MAKE TO IMPROVE IN THIS AREA?

REFLECTION ON YOUR TEACHING SKILLS - JOURNAL

DAY 48

DATE:-   /   /

1: HOW DISTRACTED DID YOU FIND YOURSELF TODAY WHY WAS THIS? HOW COULD YOU CHANGE THIS FOR THE NEXT LESSON?

2: HOW MOTIVATED WERE YOU TODAY, WHY WAS THIS AND WHAT COULD YOU DO TO IMPROVE THIS?

3: HOW GOOD WERE YOUR COMMUNICATION SKILLS TODAY? WHAT WOULD YOU LIKE TO BE DIFFERENT & HOW CAN YOU START THE CHANGE?

4: WERE YOU PATIENT TODAY? HOW DIFFERENT DO YOU FIND YOURSELF WITH DIFFERENT STUDENTS AND CLASSES? THEN LOOK AT WHY YOU MAY BE DIFFERENT?

REFLECTION ON YOUR TEACHING SKILLS - JOURNAL

 DAY 48

5: WERE YOU ABLE TO DEAL WITH ANY CONFLICT TODAY BOTH STUDENTS AND PEERS? VERY USEFUL TO LOOK AT THIS AREA WITHIN YOURSELF AND WHAT YOU COULD DO DIFFERENTLY.

6: HOW ORGANISED WERE YOU TODAY, TOO MUCH OR TOO LITTLE? WHAT WOULD YOU LIKE TO BE DIFFERENT AND HOW YOU ARE GOING TO DEAL WITH THIS DIFFERENTLY?

7: WERE YOU ENTHUSIASTIC TODAY? HOW DID THE CLASS RESPOND TO YOUR ENTHUSIASM? HOW COULD YOU DEVELOP THIS FURTHER?

8: WERE YOU CONFIDENT TODAY, HOW CONFIDENT ARE YOU ALREADY? COULD THIS BE BETTER WITHIN YOUR STUDENTS AND PEERS.

9: HOW SUPPORTIVE HAVE YOU BEEN TODAY, WHY WAS THIS? WHAT IMPROVEMENTS COULD YOU MAKE TO IMPROVE IN THIS AREA?

REFLECTION ON YOUR TEACHING SKILLS - JOURNAL

DAY 49

DATE:-   /   /

1: HOW DISTRACTED DID YOU FIND YOURSELF TODAY WHY WAS THIS? HOW COULD YOU CHANGE THIS FOR THE NEXT LESSON?

2: HOW MOTIVATED WERE YOU TODAY, WHY WAS THIS AND WHAT COULD YOU DO TO IMPROVE THIS?

3: HOW GOOD WERE YOUR COMMUNICATION SKILLS TODAY? WHAT WOULD YOU LIKE TO BE DIFFERENT & HOW CAN YOU START THE CHANGE?

4: WERE YOU PATIENT TODAY? HOW DIFFERENT DO YOU FIND YOURSELF WITH DIFFERENT STUDENTS AND CLASSES? THEN LOOK AT WHY YOU MAY BE DIFFERENT?

REFLECTION ON YOUR TEACHING SKILLS - JOURNAL

 DAY 49

5: WERE YOU ABLE TO DEAL WITH ANY CONFLICT TODAY BOTH STUDENTS AND PEERS? VERY USEFUL TO LOOK AT THIS AREA WITHIN YOURSELF AND WHAT YOU COULD DO DIFFERENTLY.

6: HOW ORGANISED WERE YOU TODAY, TOO MUCH OR TOO LITTLE? WHAT WOULD YOU LIKE TO BE DIFFERENT AND HOW YOU ARE GOING TO DEAL WITH THIS DIFFERENTLY?

7: WERE YOU ENTHUSIASTIC TODAY? HOW DID THE CLASS RESPOND TO YOUR ENTHUSIASM? HOW COULD YOU DEVELOP THIS FURTHER?

8: WERE YOU CONFIDENT TODAY, HOW CONFIDENT ARE YOU ALREADY? COULD THIS BE BETTER WITHIN YOUR STUDENTS AND PEERS.

9: HOW SUPPORTIVE HAVE YOU BEEN TODAY, WHY WAS THIS? WHAT IMPROVEMENTS COULD YOU MAKE TO IMPROVE IN THIS AREA?

REFLECTION ON YOUR TEACHING SKILLS - JOURNAL

DAY 50

DATE :-   /   /

1: HOW DISTRACTED DID YOU FIND YOURSELF TODAY WHY WAS THIS? HOW COULD YOU CHANGE THIS FOR THE NEXT LESSON?

2: HOW MOTIVATED WERE YOU TODAY, WHY WAS THIS AND WHAT COULD YOU DO TO IMPROVE THIS?

3: HOW GOOD WERE YOUR COMMUNICATION SKILLS TODAY? WHAT WOULD YOU LIKE TO BE DIFFERENT & HOW CAN YOU START THE CHANGE?

4: WERE YOU PATIENT TODAY? HOW DIFFERENT DO YOU FIND YOURSELF WITH DIFFERENT STUDENTS AND CLASSES? THEN LOOK AT WHY YOU MAY BE DIFFERENT?

REFLECTION ON YOUR TEACHING SKILLS - JOURNAL

 DAY 50

5: WERE YOU ABLE TO DEAL WITH ANY CONFLICT TODAY BOTH STUDENTS AND PEERS? VERY USEFUL TO LOOK AT THIS AREA WITHIN YOURSELF AND WHAT YOU COULD DO DIFFERENTLY.

6: HOW ORGANISED WERE YOU TODAY, TOO MUCH OR TOO LITTLE? WHAT WOULD YOU LIKE TO BE DIFFERENT AND HOW YOU ARE GOING TO DEAL WITH THIS DIFFERENTLY?

7: WERE YOU ENTHUSIASTIC TODAY? HOW DID THE CLASS RESPOND TO YOUR ENTHUSIASM? HOW COULD YOU DEVELOP THIS FURTHER?

8: WERE YOU CONFIDENT TODAY, HOW CONFIDENT ARE YOU ALREADY? COULD THIS BE BETTER WITHIN YOUR STUDENTS AND PEERS.

9: HOW SUPPORTIVE HAVE YOU BEEN TODAY, WHY WAS THIS? WHAT IMPROVEMENTS COULD YOU MAKE TO IMPROVE IN THIS AREA?

REFLECTION ON YOUR TEACHING SKILLS - JOURNAL

DAY 41 - 50 REVIEW

1: HOW HAVE I GROWN OVER THE LAST 10 DAYS?

2: WHAT AM I GOING TO FOCUS ON OVER THE NEXT 10 DAYS?

3: WHAT FIVE THINGS AM I POSITIVELY TAKING FROM THE LAST 10 DAYS AND MOVING THEM FORWARD INTO THE NEXT 10 DAYS.

-
-
-
-
-

4: WHAT KEY AREAS WOULD I LIKE TO CONCENTRATE ON TO IMPROVE MY TEACHING SKILLS FURTHER?

Day 50 Congratulations

Congratulations for meeting the halfway point, tremendous effort and fantastic that you are reflecting effectively. The book is for you only, very personnel and as you reflect on the last fifty days, look at your incredible journey. Every little change is the change you need to move forward. Think about achieving your goal of improving and what will it feel like at day 100, just imagine that feeling.

REFLECTION ON YOUR TEACHING SKILLS - JOURNAL

DAY 51

DATE:-   /   /

1: HOW DISTRACTED DID YOU FIND YOURSELF TODAY WHY WAS THIS? HOW COULD YOU CHANGE THIS FOR THE NEXT LESSON?

2: HOW MOTIVATED WERE YOU TODAY, WHY WAS THIS AND WHAT COULD YOU DO TO IMPROVE THIS?

3: HOW GOOD WERE YOUR COMMUNICATION SKILLS TODAY? WHAT WOULD YOU LIKE TO BE DIFFERENT & HOW CAN YOU START THE CHANGE?

4: WERE YOU PATIENT TODAY? HOW DIFFERENT DO YOU FIND YOURSELF WITH DIFFERENT STUDENTS AND CLASSES? THEN LOOK AT WHY YOU MAY BE DIFFERENT?

REFLECTION ON YOUR TEACHING SKILLS - JOURNAL

 DAY 51

5: WERE YOU ABLE TO DEAL WITH ANY CONFLICT TODAY BOTH STUDENTS AND PEERS? VERY USEFUL TO LOOK AT THIS AREA WITHIN YOURSELF AND WHAT YOU COULD DO DIFFERENTLY.

6: HOW ORGANISED WERE YOU TODAY, TOO MUCH OR TOO LITTLE? WHAT WOULD YOU LIKE TO BE DIFFERENT AND HOW YOU ARE GOING TO DEAL WITH THIS DIFFERENTLY?

7: WERE YOU ENTHUSIASTIC TODAY? HOW DID THE CLASS RESPOND TO YOUR ENTHUSIASM? HOW COULD YOU DEVELOP THIS FURTHER?

8: WERE YOU CONFIDENT TODAY, HOW CONFIDENT ARE YOU ALREADY? COULD THIS BE BETTER WITHIN YOUR STUDENTS AND PEERS.

9: HOW SUPPORTIVE HAVE YOU BEEN TODAY, WHY WAS THIS? WHAT IMPROVEMENTS COULD YOU MAKE TO IMPROVE IN THIS AREA?

REFLECTION ON YOUR TEACHING SKILLS - JOURNAL

DAY 52

DATE :-   /   /

1: HOW DISTRACTED DID YOU FIND YOURSELF TODAY WHY WAS THIS? HOW COULD YOU CHANGE THIS FOR THE NEXT LESSON?

2: HOW MOTIVATED WERE YOU TODAY, WHY WAS THIS AND WHAT COULD YOU DO TO IMPROVE THIS?

3: HOW GOOD WERE YOUR COMMUNICATION SKILLS TODAY? WHAT WOULD YOU LIKE TO BE DIFFERENT & HOW CAN YOU START THE CHANGE?

4: WERE YOU PATIENT TODAY? HOW DIFFERENT DO YOU FIND YOURSELF WITH DIFFERENT STUDENTS AND CLASSES? THEN LOOK AT WHY YOU MAY BE DIFFERENT?

REFLECTION ON YOUR TEACHING SKILLS - JOURNAL

 DAY 52

5: WERE YOU ABLE TO DEAL WITH ANY CONFLICT TODAY BOTH STUDENTS AND PEERS? VERY USEFUL TO LOOK AT THIS AREA WITHIN YOURSELF AND WHAT YOU COULD DO DIFFERENTLY.

6: HOW ORGANISED WERE YOU TODAY, TOO MUCH OR TOO LITTLE? WHAT WOULD YOU LIKE TO BE DIFFERENT AND HOW YOU ARE GOING TO DEAL WITH THIS DIFFERENTLY?

7: WERE YOU ENTHUSIASTIC TODAY? HOW DID THE CLASS RESPOND TO YOUR ENTHUSIASM? HOW COULD YOU DEVELOP THIS FURTHER?

8: WERE YOU CONFIDENT TODAY, HOW CONFIDENT ARE YOU ALREADY? COULD THIS BE BETTER WITHIN YOUR STUDENTS AND PEERS.

9: HOW SUPPORTIVE HAVE YOU BEEN TODAY, WHY WAS THIS? WHAT IMPROVEMENTS COULD YOU MAKE TO IMPROVE IN THIS AREA?

REFLECTION ON YOUR TEACHING SKILLS - JOURNAL

DAY 53

DATE:-   /   /

1: HOW DISTRACTED DID YOU FIND YOURSELF TODAY WHY WAS THIS? HOW COULD YOU CHANGE THIS FOR THE NEXT LESSON?

2: HOW MOTIVATED WERE YOU TODAY, WHY WAS THIS AND WHAT COULD YOU DO TO IMPROVE THIS?

3: HOW GOOD WERE YOUR COMMUNICATION SKILLS TODAY? WHAT WOULD YOU LIKE TO BE DIFFERENT & HOW CAN YOU START THE CHANGE?

4: WERE YOU PATIENT TODAY? HOW DIFFERENT DO YOU FIND YOURSELF WITH DIFFERENT STUDENTS AND CLASSES? THEN LOOK AT WHY YOU MAY BE DIFFERENT?

REFLECTION ON YOUR TEACHING SKILLS - JOURNAL

 DAY 53

5: WERE YOU ABLE TO DEAL WITH ANY CONFLICT TODAY BOTH STUDENTS AND PEERS? VERY USEFUL TO LOOK AT THIS AREA WITHIN YOURSELF AND WHAT YOU COULD DO DIFFERENTLY.

6: HOW ORGANISED WERE YOU TODAY, TOO MUCH OR TOO LITTLE? WHAT WOULD YOU LIKE TO BE DIFFERENT AND HOW YOU ARE GOING TO DEAL WITH THIS DIFFERENTLY?

7: WERE YOU ENTHUSIASTIC TODAY? HOW DID THE CLASS RESPOND TO YOUR ENTHUSIASM? HOW COULD YOU DEVELOP THIS FURTHER?

8: WERE YOU CONFIDENT TODAY, HOW CONFIDENT ARE YOU ALREADY? COULD THIS BE BETTER WITHIN YOUR STUDENTS AND PEERS.

9: HOW SUPPORTIVE HAVE YOU BEEN TODAY, WHY WAS THIS? WHAT IMPROVEMENTS COULD YOU MAKE TO IMPROVE IN THIS AREA?

REFLECTION ON YOUR TEACHING SKILLS - JOURNAL

DAY 54

DATE:-   /   /

1: HOW DISTRACTED DID YOU FIND YOURSELF TODAY WHY WAS THIS? HOW COULD YOU CHANGE THIS FOR THE NEXT LESSON?

2: HOW MOTIVATED WERE YOU TODAY, WHY WAS THIS AND WHAT COULD YOU DO TO IMPROVE THIS?

3: HOW GOOD WERE YOUR COMMUNICATION SKILLS TODAY? WHAT WOULD YOU LIKE TO BE DIFFERENT & HOW CAN YOU START THE CHANGE?

4: WERE YOU PATIENT TODAY? HOW DIFFERENT DO YOU FIND YOURSELF WITH DIFFERENT STUDENTS AND CLASSES? THEN LOOK AT WHY YOU MAY BE DIFFERENT?

REFLECTION ON YOUR TEACHING SKILLS - JOURNAL

 DAY 54

5: WERE YOU ABLE TO DEAL WITH ANY CONFLICT TODAY BOTH STUDENTS AND PEERS? VERY USEFUL TO LOOK AT THIS AREA WITHIN YOURSELF AND WHAT YOU COULD DO DIFFERENTLY.

6: HOW ORGANISED WERE YOU TODAY, TOO MUCH OR TOO LITTLE? WHAT WOULD YOU LIKE TO BE DIFFERENT AND HOW YOU ARE GOING TO DEAL WITH THIS DIFFERENTLY?

7: WERE YOU ENTHUSIASTIC TODAY? HOW DID THE CLASS RESPOND TO YOUR ENTHUSIASM? HOW COULD YOU DEVELOP THIS FURTHER?

8: WERE YOU CONFIDENT TODAY, HOW CONFIDENT ARE YOU ALREADY? COULD THIS BE BETTER WITHIN YOUR STUDENTS AND PEERS.

9: HOW SUPPORTIVE HAVE YOU BEEN TODAY, WHY WAS THIS? WHAT IMPROVEMENTS COULD YOU MAKE TO IMPROVE IN THIS AREA?

REFLECTION ON YOUR TEACHING SKILLS - JOURNAL

DAY 55

DATE:-   /   /

1: HOW DISTRACTED DID YOU FIND YOURSELF TODAY WHY WAS THIS? HOW COULD YOU CHANGE THIS FOR THE NEXT LESSON?

2: HOW MOTIVATED WERE YOU TODAY, WHY WAS THIS AND WHAT COULD YOU DO TO IMPROVE THIS?

3: HOW GOOD WERE YOUR COMMUNICATION SKILLS TODAY? WHAT WOULD YOU LIKE TO BE DIFFERENT & HOW CAN YOU START THE CHANGE?

4: WERE YOU PATIENT TODAY? HOW DIFFERENT DO YOU FIND YOURSELF WITH DIFFERENT STUDENTS AND CLASSES? THEN LOOK AT WHY YOU MAY BE DIFFERENT?

REFLECTION ON YOUR TEACHING SKILLS - JOURNAL  DAY 55

5: WERE YOU ABLE TO DEAL WITH ANY CONFLICT TODAY BOTH STUDENTS AND PEERS? VERY USEFUL TO LOOK AT THIS AREA WITHIN YOURSELF AND WHAT YOU COULD DO DIFFERENTLY.

6: HOW ORGANISED WERE YOU TODAY, TOO MUCH OR TOO LITTLE? WHAT WOULD YOU LIKE TO BE DIFFERENT AND HOW YOU ARE GOING TO DEAL WITH THIS DIFFERENTLY?

7: WERE YOU ENTHUSIASTIC TODAY? HOW DID THE CLASS RESPOND TO YOUR ENTHUSIASM? HOW COULD YOU DEVELOP THIS FURTHER?

8: WERE YOU CONFIDENT TODAY, HOW CONFIDENT ARE YOU ALREADY? COULD THIS BE BETTER WITHIN YOUR STUDENTS AND PEERS.

9: HOW SUPPORTIVE HAVE YOU BEEN TODAY, WHY WAS THIS? WHAT IMPROVEMENTS COULD YOU MAKE TO IMPROVE IN THIS AREA?

REFLECTION ON YOUR TEACHING SKILLS - JOURNAL

DAY 56

DATE:-   /   /

1: HOW DISTRACTED DID YOU FIND YOURSELF TODAY WHY WAS THIS? HOW COULD YOU CHANGE THIS FOR THE NEXT LESSON?

2: HOW MOTIVATED WERE YOU TODAY, WHY WAS THIS AND WHAT COULD YOU DO TO IMPROVE THIS?

3: HOW GOOD WERE YOUR COMMUNICATION SKILLS TODAY? WHAT WOULD YOU LIKE TO BE DIFFERENT & HOW CAN YOU START THE CHANGE?

4: WERE YOU PATIENT TODAY? HOW DIFFERENT DO YOU FIND YOURSELF WITH DIFFERENT STUDENTS AND CLASSES? THEN LOOK AT WHY YOU MAY BE DIFFERENT?

REFLECTION ON YOUR TEACHING SKILLS - JOURNAL

 DAY 56

5: WERE YOU ABLE TO DEAL WITH ANY CONFLICT TODAY BOTH STUDENTS AND PEERS? VERY USEFUL TO LOOK AT THIS AREA WITHIN YOURSELF AND WHAT YOU COULD DO DIFFERENTLY.

6: HOW ORGANISED WERE YOU TODAY, TOO MUCH OR TOO LITTLE? WHAT WOULD YOU LIKE TO BE DIFFERENT AND HOW YOU ARE GOING TO DEAL WITH THIS DIFFERENTLY?

7: WERE YOU ENTHUSIASTIC TODAY? HOW DID THE CLASS RESPOND TO YOUR ENTHUSIASM? HOW COULD YOU DEVELOP THIS FURTHER?

8: WERE YOU CONFIDENT TODAY, HOW CONFIDENT ARE YOU ALREADY? COULD THIS BE BETTER WITHIN YOUR STUDENTS AND PEERS.

9: HOW SUPPORTIVE HAVE YOU BEEN TODAY, WHY WAS THIS? WHAT IMPROVEMENTS COULD YOU MAKE TO IMPROVE IN THIS AREA?

REFLECTION ON YOUR TEACHING SKILLS - JOURNAL

DAY 57

DATE:-   /   /

1: HOW DISTRACTED DID YOU FIND YOURSELF TODAY WHY WAS THIS? HOW COULD YOU CHANGE THIS FOR THE NEXT LESSON?

2: HOW MOTIVATED WERE YOU TODAY, WHY WAS THIS AND WHAT COULD YOU DO TO IMPROVE THIS?

3: HOW GOOD WERE YOUR COMMUNICATION SKILLS TODAY? WHAT WOULD YOU LIKE TO BE DIFFERENT & HOW CAN YOU START THE CHANGE?

4: WERE YOU PATIENT TODAY? HOW DIFFERENT DO YOU FIND YOURSELF WITH DIFFERENT STUDENTS AND CLASSES? THEN LOOK AT WHY YOU MAY BE DIFFERENT?

REFLECTION ON YOUR TEACHING SKILLS - JOURNAL

 DAY 57

5: WERE YOU ABLE TO DEAL WITH ANY CONFLICT TODAY BOTH STUDENTS AND PEERS? VERY USEFUL TO LOOK AT THIS AREA WITHIN YOURSELF AND WHAT YOU COULD DO DIFFERENTLY.

6: HOW ORGANISED WERE YOU TODAY, TOO MUCH OR TOO LITTLE? WHAT WOULD YOU LIKE TO BE DIFFERENT AND HOW YOU ARE GOING TO DEAL WITH THIS DIFFERENTLY?

7: WERE YOU ENTHUSIASTIC TODAY? HOW DID THE CLASS RESPOND TO YOUR ENTHUSIASM? HOW COULD YOU DEVELOP THIS FURTHER?

8: WERE YOU CONFIDENT TODAY, HOW CONFIDENT ARE YOU ALREADY? COULD THIS BE BETTER WITHIN YOUR STUDENTS AND PEERS.

9: HOW SUPPORTIVE HAVE YOU BEEN TODAY, WHY WAS THIS? WHAT IMPROVEMENTS COULD YOU MAKE TO IMPROVE IN THIS AREA?

REFLECTION ON YOUR TEACHING SKILLS - JOURNAL

DAY 58

DATE:-   /   /

1: HOW DISTRACTED DID YOU FIND YOURSELF TODAY WHY WAS THIS? HOW COULD YOU CHANGE THIS FOR THE NEXT LESSON?

2: HOW MOTIVATED WERE YOU TODAY, WHY WAS THIS AND WHAT COULD YOU DO TO IMPROVE THIS?

3: HOW GOOD WERE YOUR COMMUNICATION SKILLS TODAY? WHAT WOULD YOU LIKE TO BE DIFFERENT & HOW CAN YOU START THE CHANGE?

4: WERE YOU PATIENT TODAY? HOW DIFFERENT DO YOU FIND YOURSELF WITH DIFFERENT STUDENTS AND CLASSES? THEN LOOK AT WHY YOU MAY BE DIFFERENT?

REFLECTION ON YOUR TEACHING SKILLS - JOURNAL

 DAY 58

5: WERE YOU ABLE TO DEAL WITH ANY CONFLICT TODAY BOTH STUDENTS AND PEERS? VERY USEFUL TO LOOK AT THIS AREA WITHIN YOURSELF AND WHAT YOU COULD DO DIFFERENTLY.

6: HOW ORGANISED WERE YOU TODAY, TOO MUCH OR TOO LITTLE? WHAT WOULD YOU LIKE TO BE DIFFERENT AND HOW YOU ARE GOING TO DEAL WITH THIS DIFFERENTLY?

7: WERE YOU ENTHUSIASTIC TODAY? HOW DID THE CLASS RESPOND TO YOUR ENTHUSIASM? HOW COULD YOU DEVELOP THIS FURTHER?

8: WERE YOU CONFIDENT TODAY, HOW CONFIDENT ARE YOU ALREADY? COULD THIS BE BETTER WITHIN YOUR STUDENTS AND PEERS.

9: HOW SUPPORTIVE HAVE YOU BEEN TODAY, WHY WAS THIS? WHAT IMPROVEMENTS COULD YOU MAKE TO IMPROVE IN THIS AREA?

REFLECTION ON YOUR TEACHING SKILLS - JOURNAL

DAY 59

DATE:-   /   /

1: HOW DISTRACTED DID YOU FIND YOURSELF TODAY WHY WAS THIS? HOW COULD YOU CHANGE THIS FOR THE NEXT LESSON?

2: HOW MOTIVATED WERE YOU TODAY, WHY WAS THIS AND WHAT COULD YOU DO TO IMPROVE THIS?

3: HOW GOOD WERE YOUR COMMUNICATION SKILLS TODAY? WHAT WOULD YOU LIKE TO BE DIFFERENT & HOW CAN YOU START THE CHANGE?

4: WERE YOU PATIENT TODAY? HOW DIFFERENT DO YOU FIND YOURSELF WITH DIFFERENT STUDENTS AND CLASSES? THEN LOOK AT WHY YOU MAY BE DIFFERENT?

REFLECTION ON YOUR TEACHING SKILLS - JOURNAL

 DAY 59

5: WERE YOU ABLE TO DEAL WITH ANY CONFLICT TODAY BOTH STUDENTS AND PEERS? VERY USEFUL TO LOOK AT THIS AREA WITHIN YOURSELF AND WHAT YOU COULD DO DIFFERENTLY.

6: HOW ORGANISED WERE YOU TODAY, TOO MUCH OR TOO LITTLE? WHAT WOULD YOU LIKE TO BE DIFFERENT AND HOW YOU ARE GOING TO DEAL WITH THIS DIFFERENTLY?

7: WERE YOU ENTHUSIASTIC TODAY? HOW DID THE CLASS RESPOND TO YOUR ENTHUSIASM? HOW COULD YOU DEVELOP THIS FURTHER?

8: WERE YOU CONFIDENT TODAY, HOW CONFIDENT ARE YOU ALREADY? COULD THIS BE BETTER WITHIN YOUR STUDENTS AND PEERS.

9: HOW SUPPORTIVE HAVE YOU BEEN TODAY, WHY WAS THIS? WHAT IMPROVEMENTS COULD YOU MAKE TO IMPROVE IN THIS AREA?

REFLECTION ON YOUR TEACHING SKILLS - JOURNAL

DAY 60

DATE:-   /   /

1: HOW DISTRACTED DID YOU FIND YOURSELF TODAY WHY WAS THIS? HOW COULD YOU CHANGE THIS FOR THE NEXT LESSON?

2: HOW MOTIVATED WERE YOU TODAY, WHY WAS THIS AND WHAT COULD YOU DO TO IMPROVE THIS?

3: HOW GOOD WERE YOUR COMMUNICATION SKILLS TODAY? WHAT WOULD YOU LIKE TO BE DIFFERENT & HOW CAN YOU START THE CHANGE?

4: WERE YOU PATIENT TODAY? HOW DIFFERENT DO YOU FIND YOURSELF WITH DIFFERENT STUDENTS AND CLASSES? THEN LOOK AT WHY YOU MAY BE DIFFERENT?

REFLECTION ON YOUR TEACHING SKILLS - JOURNAL

 DAY 60

5: WERE YOU ABLE TO DEAL WITH ANY CONFLICT TODAY BOTH STUDENTS AND PEERS? VERY USEFUL TO LOOK AT THIS AREA WITHIN YOURSELF AND WHAT YOU COULD DO DIFFERENTLY.

6: HOW ORGANISED WERE YOU TODAY, TOO MUCH OR TOO LITTLE? WHAT WOULD YOU LIKE TO BE DIFFERENT AND HOW YOU ARE GOING TO DEAL WITH THIS DIFFERENTLY?

7: WERE YOU ENTHUSIASTIC TODAY? HOW DID THE CLASS RESPOND TO YOUR ENTHUSIASM? HOW COULD YOU DEVELOP THIS FURTHER?

8: WERE YOU CONFIDENT TODAY, HOW CONFIDENT ARE YOU ALREADY? COULD THIS BE BETTER WITHIN YOUR STUDENTS AND PEERS.

9: HOW SUPPORTIVE HAVE YOU BEEN TODAY, WHY WAS THIS? WHAT IMPROVEMENTS COULD YOU MAKE TO IMPROVE IN THIS AREA?

REFLECTION ON YOUR TEACHING SKILLS - JOURNAL

DAY 51 - 60 REVIEW

1: HOW HAVE I GROWN OVER THE LAST 10 DAYS?

2: WHAT AM I GOING TO FOCUS ON OVER THE NEXT 10 DAYS?

3: WHAT FIVE THINGS AM I POSITIVELY TAKING FROM THE LAST 10 DAYS AND MOVING THEM FORWARD INTO THE NEXT 10 DAYS.

-
-
-
-
-

4: WHAT KEY AREAS WOULD I LIKE TO CONCENTRATE ON TO IMPROVE MY TEACHING SKILLS FURTHER?

> "A good teacher must be able to put himself in the place of those who find learning hard."

REFLECTION ON YOUR TEACHING SKILLS - JOURNAL

DAY 61

DATE:-   /   /

1: HOW DISTRACTED DID YOU FIND YOURSELF TODAY WHY WAS THIS? HOW COULD YOU CHANGE THIS FOR THE NEXT LESSON?

2: HOW MOTIVATED WERE YOU TODAY, WHY WAS THIS AND WHAT COULD YOU DO TO IMPROVE THIS?

3: HOW GOOD WERE YOUR COMMUNICATION SKILLS TODAY? WHAT WOULD YOU LIKE TO BE DIFFERENT & HOW CAN YOU START THE CHANGE?

4: WERE YOU PATIENT TODAY? HOW DIFFERENT DO YOU FIND YOURSELF WITH DIFFERENT STUDENTS AND CLASSES? THEN LOOK AT WHY YOU MAY BE DIFFERENT?

REFLECTION ON YOUR TEACHING SKILLS - JOURNAL

 DAY 61

5: WERE YOU ABLE TO DEAL WITH ANY CONFLICT TODAY BOTH STUDENTS AND PEERS? VERY USEFUL TO LOOK AT THIS AREA WITHIN YOURSELF AND WHAT YOU COULD DO DIFFERENTLY.

6: HOW ORGANISED WERE YOU TODAY, TOO MUCH OR TOO LITTLE? WHAT WOULD YOU LIKE TO BE DIFFERENT AND HOW YOU ARE GOING TO DEAL WITH THIS DIFFERENTLY?

7: WERE YOU ENTHUSIASTIC TODAY? HOW DID THE CLASS RESPOND TO YOUR ENTHUSIASM? HOW COULD YOU DEVELOP THIS FURTHER?

8: WERE YOU CONFIDENT TODAY, HOW CONFIDENT ARE YOU ALREADY? COULD THIS BE BETTER WITHIN YOUR STUDENTS AND PEERS.

9: HOW SUPPORTIVE HAVE YOU BEEN TODAY, WHY WAS THIS? WHAT IMPROVEMENTS COULD YOU MAKE TO IMPROVE IN THIS AREA?

REFLECTION ON YOUR TEACHING SKILLS - JOURNAL

DAY 62

DATE:-   /   /

1: HOW DISTRACTED DID YOU FIND YOURSELF TODAY WHY WAS THIS? HOW COULD YOU CHANGE THIS FOR THE NEXT LESSON?

2: HOW MOTIVATED WERE YOU TODAY, WHY WAS THIS AND WHAT COULD YOU DO TO IMPROVE THIS?

3: HOW GOOD WERE YOUR COMMUNICATION SKILLS TODAY? WHAT WOULD YOU LIKE TO BE DIFFERENT & HOW CAN YOU START THE CHANGE?

4: WERE YOU PATIENT TODAY? HOW DIFFERENT DO YOU FIND YOURSELF WITH DIFFERENT STUDENTS AND CLASSES? THEN LOOK AT WHY YOU MAY BE DIFFERENT?

REFLECTION ON YOUR TEACHING SKILLS - JOURNAL

 DAY 62

5: WERE YOU ABLE TO DEAL WITH ANY CONFLICT TODAY BOTH STUDENTS AND PEERS? VERY USEFUL TO LOOK AT THIS AREA WITHIN YOURSELF AND WHAT YOU COULD DO DIFFERENTLY.

6: HOW ORGANISED WERE YOU TODAY, TOO MUCH OR TOO LITTLE? WHAT WOULD YOU LIKE TO BE DIFFERENT AND HOW YOU ARE GOING TO DEAL WITH THIS DIFFERENTLY?

7: WERE YOU ENTHUSIASTIC TODAY? HOW DID THE CLASS RESPOND TO YOUR ENTHUSIASM? HOW COULD YOU DEVELOP THIS FURTHER?

8: WERE YOU CONFIDENT TODAY, HOW CONFIDENT ARE YOU ALREADY? COULD THIS BE BETTER WITHIN YOUR STUDENTS AND PEERS.

9: HOW SUPPORTIVE HAVE YOU BEEN TODAY, WHY WAS THIS? WHAT IMPROVEMENTS COULD YOU MAKE TO IMPROVE IN THIS AREA?

REFLECTION ON YOUR TEACHING SKILLS - JOURNAL

DAY 63

DATE:-   /   /

1: HOW DISTRACTED DID YOU FIND YOURSELF TODAY WHY WAS THIS? HOW COULD YOU CHANGE THIS FOR THE NEXT LESSON?

2: HOW MOTIVATED WERE YOU TODAY, WHY WAS THIS AND WHAT COULD YOU DO TO IMPROVE THIS?

3: HOW GOOD WERE YOUR COMMUNICATION SKILLS TODAY? WHAT WOULD YOU LIKE TO BE DIFFERENT & HOW CAN YOU START THE CHANGE?

4: WERE YOU PATIENT TODAY? HOW DIFFERENT DO YOU FIND YOURSELF WITH DIFFERENT STUDENTS AND CLASSES? THEN LOOK AT WHY YOU MAY BE DIFFERENT?

REFLECTION ON YOUR TEACHING SKILLS - JOURNAL

 DAY 63

5: WERE YOU ABLE TO DEAL WITH ANY CONFLICT TODAY BOTH STUDENTS AND PEERS? VERY USEFUL TO LOOK AT THIS AREA WITHIN YOURSELF AND WHAT YOU COULD DO DIFFERENTLY.

6: HOW ORGANISED WERE YOU TODAY, TOO MUCH OR TOO LITTLE? WHAT WOULD YOU LIKE TO BE DIFFERENT AND HOW YOU ARE GOING TO DEAL WITH THIS DIFFERENTLY?

7: WERE YOU ENTHUSIASTIC TODAY? HOW DID THE CLASS RESPOND TO YOUR ENTHUSIASM? HOW COULD YOU DEVELOP THIS FURTHER?

8: WERE YOU CONFIDENT TODAY, HOW CONFIDENT ARE YOU ALREADY? COULD THIS BE BETTER WITHIN YOUR STUDENTS AND PEERS.

9: HOW SUPPORTIVE HAVE YOU BEEN TODAY, WHY WAS THIS? WHAT IMPROVEMENTS COULD YOU MAKE TO IMPROVE IN THIS AREA?

REFLECTION ON YOUR TEACHING SKILLS - JOURNAL

DAY 64

DATE:-   /   /

1: HOW DISTRACTED DID YOU FIND YOURSELF TODAY WHY WAS THIS? HOW COULD YOU CHANGE THIS FOR THE NEXT LESSON?

2: HOW MOTIVATED WERE YOU TODAY, WHY WAS THIS AND WHAT COULD YOU DO TO IMPROVE THIS?

3: HOW GOOD WERE YOUR COMMUNICATION SKILLS TODAY? WHAT WOULD YOU LIKE TO BE DIFFERENT & HOW CAN YOU START THE CHANGE?

4: WERE YOU PATIENT TODAY? HOW DIFFERENT DO YOU FIND YOURSELF WITH DIFFERENT STUDENTS AND CLASSES? THEN LOOK AT WHY YOU MAY BE DIFFERENT?

REFLECTION ON YOUR TEACHING SKILLS - JOURNAL

 DAY 64

5: WERE YOU ABLE TO DEAL WITH ANY CONFLICT TODAY BOTH STUDENTS AND PEERS? VERY USEFUL TO LOOK AT THIS AREA WITHIN YOURSELF AND WHAT YOU COULD DO DIFFERENTLY.

6: HOW ORGANISED WERE YOU TODAY, TOO MUCH OR TOO LITTLE? WHAT WOULD YOU LIKE TO BE DIFFERENT AND HOW YOU ARE GOING TO DEAL WITH THIS DIFFERENTLY?

7: WERE YOU ENTHUSIASTIC TODAY? HOW DID THE CLASS RESPOND TO YOUR ENTHUSIASM? HOW COULD YOU DEVELOP THIS FURTHER?

8: WERE YOU CONFIDENT TODAY, HOW CONFIDENT ARE YOU ALREADY? COULD THIS BE BETTER WITHIN YOUR STUDENTS AND PEERS.

9: HOW SUPPORTIVE HAVE YOU BEEN TODAY, WHY WAS THIS? WHAT IMPROVEMENTS COULD YOU MAKE TO IMPROVE IN THIS AREA?

REFLECTION ON YOUR TEACHING SKILLS - JOURNAL

DAY 65

DATE:-   /   /

1: HOW DISTRACTED DID YOU FIND YOURSELF TODAY WHY WAS THIS? HOW COULD YOU CHANGE THIS FOR THE NEXT LESSON?

2: HOW MOTIVATED WERE YOU TODAY, WHY WAS THIS AND WHAT COULD YOU DO TO IMPROVE THIS?

3: HOW GOOD WERE YOUR COMMUNICATION SKILLS TODAY? WHAT WOULD YOU LIKE TO BE DIFFERENT & HOW CAN YOU START THE CHANGE?

4: WERE YOU PATIENT TODAY? HOW DIFFERENT DO YOU FIND YOURSELF WITH DIFFERENT STUDENTS AND CLASSES? THEN LOOK AT WHY YOU MAY BE DIFFERENT?

REFLECTION ON YOUR TEACHING SKILLS - JOURNAL

 DAY 65

5: WERE YOU ABLE TO DEAL WITH ANY CONFLICT TODAY BOTH STUDENTS AND PEERS? VERY USEFUL TO LOOK AT THIS AREA WITHIN YOURSELF AND WHAT YOU COULD DO DIFFERENTLY.

6: HOW ORGANISED WERE YOU TODAY, TOO MUCH OR TOO LITTLE? WHAT WOULD YOU LIKE TO BE DIFFERENT AND HOW YOU ARE GOING TO DEAL WITH THIS DIFFERENTLY?

7: WERE YOU ENTHUSIASTIC TODAY? HOW DID THE CLASS RESPOND TO YOUR ENTHUSIASM? HOW COULD YOU DEVELOP THIS FURTHER?

8: WERE YOU CONFIDENT TODAY, HOW CONFIDENT ARE YOU ALREADY? COULD THIS BE BETTER WITHIN YOUR STUDENTS AND PEERS.

9: HOW SUPPORTIVE HAVE YOU BEEN TODAY, WHY WAS THIS? WHAT IMPROVEMENTS COULD YOU MAKE TO IMPROVE IN THIS AREA?

REFLECTION ON YOUR TEACHING SKILLS - JOURNAL

DAY 66

DATE:-   /   /

1: HOW DISTRACTED DID YOU FIND YOURSELF TODAY WHY WAS THIS? HOW COULD YOU CHANGE THIS FOR THE NEXT LESSON?

2: HOW MOTIVATED WERE YOU TODAY, WHY WAS THIS AND WHAT COULD YOU DO TO IMPROVE THIS?

3: HOW GOOD WERE YOUR COMMUNICATION SKILLS TODAY? WHAT WOULD YOU LIKE TO BE DIFFERENT & HOW CAN YOU START THE CHANGE?

4: WERE YOU PATIENT TODAY? HOW DIFFERENT DO YOU FIND YOURSELF WITH DIFFERENT STUDENTS AND CLASSES? THEN LOOK AT WHY YOU MAY BE DIFFERENT?

REFLECTION ON YOUR TEACHING SKILLS - JOURNAL

 DAY 66

5: WERE YOU ABLE TO DEAL WITH ANY CONFLICT TODAY BOTH STUDENTS AND PEERS? VERY USEFUL TO LOOK AT THIS AREA WITHIN YOURSELF AND WHAT YOU COULD DO DIFFERENTLY.

6: HOW ORGANISED WERE YOU TODAY, TOO MUCH OR TOO LITTLE? WHAT WOULD YOU LIKE TO BE DIFFERENT AND HOW YOU ARE GOING TO DEAL WITH THIS DIFFERENTLY?

7: WERE YOU ENTHUSIASTIC TODAY? HOW DID THE CLASS RESPOND TO YOUR ENTHUSIASM? HOW COULD YOU DEVELOP THIS FURTHER?

8: WERE YOU CONFIDENT TODAY, HOW CONFIDENT ARE YOU ALREADY? COULD THIS BE BETTER WITHIN YOUR STUDENTS AND PEERS.

9: HOW SUPPORTIVE HAVE YOU BEEN TODAY, WHY WAS THIS? WHAT IMPROVEMENTS COULD YOU MAKE TO IMPROVE IN THIS AREA?

REFLECTION ON YOUR TEACHING SKILLS - JOURNAL

DAY 67

DATE:-   /   /

1: HOW DISTRACTED DID YOU FIND YOURSELF TODAY WHY WAS THIS? HOW COULD YOU CHANGE THIS FOR THE NEXT LESSON?

2: HOW MOTIVATED WERE YOU TODAY, WHY WAS THIS AND WHAT COULD YOU DO TO IMPROVE THIS?

3: HOW GOOD WERE YOUR COMMUNICATION SKILLS TODAY? WHAT WOULD YOU LIKE TO BE DIFFERENT & HOW CAN YOU START THE CHANGE?

4: WERE YOU PATIENT TODAY? HOW DIFFERENT DO YOU FIND YOURSELF WITH DIFFERENT STUDENTS AND CLASSES? THEN LOOK AT WHY YOU MAY BE DIFFERENT?

REFLECTION ON YOUR TEACHING SKILLS - JOURNAL  DAY 67

5: WERE YOU ABLE TO DEAL WITH ANY CONFLICT TODAY BOTH STUDENTS AND PEERS? VERY USEFUL TO LOOK AT THIS AREA WITHIN YOURSELF AND WHAT YOU COULD DO DIFFERENTLY.

6: HOW ORGANISED WERE YOU TODAY, TOO MUCH OR TOO LITTLE? WHAT WOULD YOU LIKE TO BE DIFFERENT AND HOW YOU ARE GOING TO DEAL WITH THIS DIFFERENTLY?

7: WERE YOU ENTHUSIASTIC TODAY? HOW DID THE CLASS RESPOND TO YOUR ENTHUSIASM? HOW COULD YOU DEVELOP THIS FURTHER?

8: WERE YOU CONFIDENT TODAY, HOW CONFIDENT ARE YOU ALREADY? COULD THIS BE BETTER WITHIN YOUR STUDENTS AND PEERS.

9: HOW SUPPORTIVE HAVE YOU BEEN TODAY, WHY WAS THIS? WHAT IMPROVEMENTS COULD YOU MAKE TO IMPROVE IN THIS AREA?

REFLECTION ON YOUR TEACHING SKILLS - JOURNAL

DAY 68

DATE:-   /   /

1: HOW DISTRACTED DID YOU FIND YOURSELF TODAY WHY WAS THIS? HOW COULD YOU CHANGE THIS FOR THE NEXT LESSON?

2: HOW MOTIVATED WERE YOU TODAY, WHY WAS THIS AND WHAT COULD YOU DO TO IMPROVE THIS?

3: HOW GOOD WERE YOUR COMMUNICATION SKILLS TODAY? WHAT WOULD YOU LIKE TO BE DIFFERENT & HOW CAN YOU START THE CHANGE?

4: WERE YOU PATIENT TODAY? HOW DIFFERENT DO YOU FIND YOURSELF WITH DIFFERENT STUDENTS AND CLASSES? THEN LOOK AT WHY YOU MAY BE DIFFERENT?

REFLECTION ON YOUR TEACHING SKILLS - JOURNAL

 DAY 68

5: WERE YOU ABLE TO DEAL WITH ANY CONFLICT TODAY BOTH STUDENTS AND PEERS? VERY USEFUL TO LOOK AT THIS AREA WITHIN YOURSELF AND WHAT YOU COULD DO DIFFERENTLY.

6: HOW ORGANISED WERE YOU TODAY, TOO MUCH OR TOO LITTLE? WHAT WOULD YOU LIKE TO BE DIFFERENT AND HOW YOU ARE GOING TO DEAL WITH THIS DIFFERENTLY?

7: WERE YOU ENTHUSIASTIC TODAY? HOW DID THE CLASS RESPOND TO YOUR ENTHUSIASM? HOW COULD YOU DEVELOP THIS FURTHER?

8: WERE YOU CONFIDENT TODAY, HOW CONFIDENT ARE YOU ALREADY? COULD THIS BE BETTER WITHIN YOUR STUDENTS AND PEERS.

9: HOW SUPPORTIVE HAVE YOU BEEN TODAY, WHY WAS THIS? WHAT IMPROVEMENTS COULD YOU MAKE TO IMPROVE IN THIS AREA?

REFLECTION ON YOUR TEACHING SKILLS - JOURNAL

DAY 69

DATE:-   /   /

1: HOW DISTRACTED DID YOU FIND YOURSELF TODAY WHY WAS THIS? HOW COULD YOU CHANGE THIS FOR THE NEXT LESSON?

2: HOW MOTIVATED WERE YOU TODAY, WHY WAS THIS AND WHAT COULD YOU DO TO IMPROVE THIS?

3: HOW GOOD WERE YOUR COMMUNICATION SKILLS TODAY? WHAT WOULD YOU LIKE TO BE DIFFERENT & HOW CAN YOU START THE CHANGE?

4: WERE YOU PATIENT TODAY? HOW DIFFERENT DO YOU FIND YOURSELF WITH DIFFERENT STUDENTS AND CLASSES? THEN LOOK AT WHY YOU MAY BE DIFFERENT?

REFLECTION ON YOUR TEACHING SKILLS - JOURNAL

 DAY 69

5: WERE YOU ABLE TO DEAL WITH ANY CONFLICT TODAY BOTH STUDENTS AND PEERS? VERY USEFUL TO LOOK AT THIS AREA WITHIN YOURSELF AND WHAT YOU COULD DO DIFFERENTLY.

6: HOW ORGANISED WERE YOU TODAY, TOO MUCH OR TOO LITTLE? WHAT WOULD YOU LIKE TO BE DIFFERENT AND HOW YOU ARE GOING TO DEAL WITH THIS DIFFERENTLY?

7: WERE YOU ENTHUSIASTIC TODAY? HOW DID THE CLASS RESPOND TO YOUR ENTHUSIASM? HOW COULD YOU DEVELOP THIS FURTHER?

8: WERE YOU CONFIDENT TODAY, HOW CONFIDENT ARE YOU ALREADY? COULD THIS BE BETTER WITHIN YOUR STUDENTS AND PEERS.

9: HOW SUPPORTIVE HAVE YOU BEEN TODAY, WHY WAS THIS? WHAT IMPROVEMENTS COULD YOU MAKE TO IMPROVE IN THIS AREA?

REFLECTION ON YOUR TEACHING SKILLS - JOURNAL

DAY 70

DATE:-   /   /

1: HOW DISTRACTED DID YOU FIND YOURSELF TODAY WHY WAS THIS? HOW COULD YOU CHANGE THIS FOR THE NEXT LESSON?

2: HOW MOTIVATED WERE YOU TODAY, WHY WAS THIS AND WHAT COULD YOU DO TO IMPROVE THIS?

3: HOW GOOD WERE YOUR COMMUNICATION SKILLS TODAY? WHAT WOULD YOU LIKE TO BE DIFFERENT & HOW CAN YOU START THE CHANGE?

4: WERE YOU PATIENT TODAY? HOW DIFFERENT DO YOU FIND YOURSELF WITH DIFFERENT STUDENTS AND CLASSES? THEN LOOK AT WHY YOU MAY BE DIFFERENT?

REFLECTION ON YOUR TEACHING SKILLS - JOURNAL

 DAY 70

5: WERE YOU ABLE TO DEAL WITH ANY CONFLICT TODAY BOTH STUDENTS AND PEERS? VERY USEFUL TO LOOK AT THIS AREA WITHIN YOURSELF AND WHAT YOU COULD DO DIFFERENTLY.

6: HOW ORGANISED WERE YOU TODAY, TOO MUCH OR TOO LITTLE? WHAT WOULD YOU LIKE TO BE DIFFERENT AND HOW YOU ARE GOING TO DEAL WITH THIS DIFFERENTLY?

7: WERE YOU ENTHUSIASTIC TODAY? HOW DID THE CLASS RESPOND TO YOUR ENTHUSIASM? HOW COULD YOU DEVELOP THIS FURTHER?

8: WERE YOU CONFIDENT TODAY, HOW CONFIDENT ARE YOU ALREADY? COULD THIS BE BETTER WITHIN YOUR STUDENTS AND PEERS.

9: HOW SUPPORTIVE HAVE YOU BEEN TODAY, WHY WAS THIS? WHAT IMPROVEMENTS COULD YOU MAKE TO IMPROVE IN THIS AREA?

REFLECTION ON YOUR TEACHING SKILLS - JOURNAL

DAY 61 - 70 REVIEW

1: HOW HAVE I GROWN OVER THE LAST 10 DAYS?

2: WHAT AM I GOING TO FOCUS ON OVER THE NEXT 10 DAYS?

3: WHAT FIVE THINGS AM I POSITIVELY TAKING FROM THE LAST 10 DAYS AND MOVING THEM FORWARD INTO THE NEXT 10 DAYS.

-
-
-
-
-

4: WHAT KEY AREAS WOULD I LIKE TO CONCENTRATE ON TO IMPROVE MY TEACHING SKILLS FURTHER?

"A good teacher can inspire hope, ignite the imagination, and instil a love of learning."

REFLECTION ON YOUR TEACHING SKILLS - JOURNAL

DAY 71

DATE:-   /   /

1: HOW DISTRACTED DID YOU FIND YOURSELF TODAY WHY WAS THIS? HOW COULD YOU CHANGE THIS FOR THE NEXT LESSON?

2: HOW MOTIVATED WERE YOU TODAY, WHY WAS THIS AND WHAT COULD YOU DO TO IMPROVE THIS?

3: HOW GOOD WERE YOUR COMMUNICATION SKILLS TODAY? WHAT WOULD YOU LIKE TO BE DIFFERENT & HOW CAN YOU START THE CHANGE?

4: WERE YOU PATIENT TODAY? HOW DIFFERENT DO YOU FIND YOURSELF WITH DIFFERENT STUDENTS AND CLASSES? THEN LOOK AT WHY YOU MAY BE DIFFERENT?

REFLECTION ON YOUR TEACHING SKILLS - JOURNAL

 DAY 71

5: WERE YOU ABLE TO DEAL WITH ANY CONFLICT TODAY BOTH STUDENTS AND PEERS? VERY USEFUL TO LOOK AT THIS AREA WITHIN YOURSELF AND WHAT YOU COULD DO DIFFERENTLY.

6: HOW ORGANISED WERE YOU TODAY, TOO MUCH OR TOO LITTLE? WHAT WOULD YOU LIKE TO BE DIFFERENT AND HOW YOU ARE GOING TO DEAL WITH THIS DIFFERENTLY?

7: WERE YOU ENTHUSIASTIC TODAY? HOW DID THE CLASS RESPOND TO YOUR ENTHUSIASM? HOW COULD YOU DEVELOP THIS FURTHER?

8: WERE YOU CONFIDENT TODAY, HOW CONFIDENT ARE YOU ALREADY? COULD THIS BE BETTER WITHIN YOUR STUDENTS AND PEERS.

9: HOW SUPPORTIVE HAVE YOU BEEN TODAY, WHY WAS THIS? WHAT IMPROVEMENTS COULD YOU MAKE TO IMPROVE IN THIS AREA?

REFLECTION ON YOUR TEACHING SKILLS - JOURNAL

DAY 72

DATE:-   /   /

1: HOW DISTRACTED DID YOU FIND YOURSELF TODAY WHY WAS THIS? HOW COULD YOU CHANGE THIS FOR THE NEXT LESSON?

2: HOW MOTIVATED WERE YOU TODAY, WHY WAS THIS AND WHAT COULD YOU DO TO IMPROVE THIS?

3: HOW GOOD WERE YOUR COMMUNICATION SKILLS TODAY? WHAT WOULD YOU LIKE TO BE DIFFERENT & HOW CAN YOU START THE CHANGE?

4: WERE YOU PATIENT TODAY? HOW DIFFERENT DO YOU FIND YOURSELF WITH DIFFERENT STUDENTS AND CLASSES? THEN LOOK AT WHY YOU MAY BE DIFFERENT?

REFLECTION ON YOUR TEACHING SKILLS - JOURNAL

 DAY 72

5: WERE YOU ABLE TO DEAL WITH ANY CONFLICT TODAY BOTH STUDENTS AND PEERS? VERY USEFUL TO LOOK AT THIS AREA WITHIN YOURSELF AND WHAT YOU COULD DO DIFFERENTLY.

6: HOW ORGANISED WERE YOU TODAY, TOO MUCH OR TOO LITTLE? WHAT WOULD YOU LIKE TO BE DIFFERENT AND HOW YOU ARE GOING TO DEAL WITH THIS DIFFERENTLY?

7: WERE YOU ENTHUSIASTIC TODAY? HOW DID THE CLASS RESPOND TO YOUR ENTHUSIASM? HOW COULD YOU DEVELOP THIS FURTHER?

8: WERE YOU CONFIDENT TODAY, HOW CONFIDENT ARE YOU ALREADY? COULD THIS BE BETTER WITHIN YOUR STUDENTS AND PEERS.

9: HOW SUPPORTIVE HAVE YOU BEEN TODAY, WHY WAS THIS? WHAT IMPROVEMENTS COULD YOU MAKE TO IMPROVE IN THIS AREA?

REFLECTION ON YOUR TEACHING SKILLS - JOURNAL

DAY 73

DATE:-   /   /

1: HOW DISTRACTED DID YOU FIND YOURSELF TODAY WHY WAS THIS? HOW COULD YOU CHANGE THIS FOR THE NEXT LESSON?

2: HOW MOTIVATED WERE YOU TODAY, WHY WAS THIS AND WHAT COULD YOU DO TO IMPROVE THIS?

3: HOW GOOD WERE YOUR COMMUNICATION SKILLS TODAY? WHAT WOULD YOU LIKE TO BE DIFFERENT & HOW CAN YOU START THE CHANGE?

4: WERE YOU PATIENT TODAY? HOW DIFFERENT DO YOU FIND YOURSELF WITH DIFFERENT STUDENTS AND CLASSES? THEN LOOK AT WHY YOU MAY BE DIFFERENT?

REFLECTION ON YOUR TEACHING SKILLS - JOURNAL

 DAY 73

5: WERE YOU ABLE TO DEAL WITH ANY CONFLICT TODAY BOTH STUDENTS AND PEERS? VERY USEFUL TO LOOK AT THIS AREA WITHIN YOURSELF AND WHAT YOU COULD DO DIFFERENTLY.

6: HOW ORGANISED WERE YOU TODAY, TOO MUCH OR TOO LITTLE? WHAT WOULD YOU LIKE TO BE DIFFERENT AND HOW YOU ARE GOING TO DEAL WITH THIS DIFFERENTLY?

7: WERE YOU ENTHUSIASTIC TODAY? HOW DID THE CLASS RESPOND TO YOUR ENTHUSIASM? HOW COULD YOU DEVELOP THIS FURTHER?

8: WERE YOU CONFIDENT TODAY, HOW CONFIDENT ARE YOU ALREADY? COULD THIS BE BETTER WITHIN YOUR STUDENTS AND PEERS.

9: HOW SUPPORTIVE HAVE YOU BEEN TODAY, WHY WAS THIS? WHAT IMPROVEMENTS COULD YOU MAKE TO IMPROVE IN THIS AREA?

REFLECTION ON YOUR TEACHING SKILLS - JOURNAL

DAY 74

DATE:-   /   /

1: HOW DISTRACTED DID YOU FIND YOURSELF TODAY WHY WAS THIS? HOW COULD YOU CHANGE THIS FOR THE NEXT LESSON?

2: HOW MOTIVATED WERE YOU TODAY, WHY WAS THIS AND WHAT COULD YOU DO TO IMPROVE THIS?

3: HOW GOOD WERE YOUR COMMUNICATION SKILLS TODAY? WHAT WOULD YOU LIKE TO BE DIFFERENT & HOW CAN YOU START THE CHANGE?

4: WERE YOU PATIENT TODAY? HOW DIFFERENT DO YOU FIND YOURSELF WITH DIFFERENT STUDENTS AND CLASSES? THEN LOOK AT WHY YOU MAY BE DIFFERENT?

REFLECTION ON YOUR TEACHING SKILLS - JOURNAL

 DAY 74

5: WERE YOU ABLE TO DEAL WITH ANY CONFLICT TODAY BOTH STUDENTS AND PEERS? VERY USEFUL TO LOOK AT THIS AREA WITHIN YOURSELF AND WHAT YOU COULD DO DIFFERENTLY.

6: HOW ORGANISED WERE YOU TODAY, TOO MUCH OR TOO LITTLE? WHAT WOULD YOU LIKE TO BE DIFFERENT AND HOW YOU ARE GOING TO DEAL WITH THIS DIFFERENTLY?

7: WERE YOU ENTHUSIASTIC TODAY? HOW DID THE CLASS RESPOND TO YOUR ENTHUSIASM? HOW COULD YOU DEVELOP THIS FURTHER?

8: WERE YOU CONFIDENT TODAY, HOW CONFIDENT ARE YOU ALREADY? COULD THIS BE BETTER WITHIN YOUR STUDENTS AND PEERS.

9: HOW SUPPORTIVE HAVE YOU BEEN TODAY, WHY WAS THIS? WHAT IMPROVEMENTS COULD YOU MAKE TO IMPROVE IN THIS AREA?

REFLECTION ON YOUR TEACHING SKILLS - JOURNAL

DAY 75

DATE:-   /   /

1: HOW DISTRACTED DID YOU FIND YOURSELF TODAY WHY WAS THIS? HOW COULD YOU CHANGE THIS FOR THE NEXT LESSON?

2: HOW MOTIVATED WERE YOU TODAY, WHY WAS THIS AND WHAT COULD YOU DO TO IMPROVE THIS?

3: HOW GOOD WERE YOUR COMMUNICATION SKILLS TODAY? WHAT WOULD YOU LIKE TO BE DIFFERENT & HOW CAN YOU START THE CHANGE?

4: WERE YOU PATIENT TODAY? HOW DIFFERENT DO YOU FIND YOURSELF WITH DIFFERENT STUDENTS AND CLASSES? THEN LOOK AT WHY YOU MAY BE DIFFERENT?

REFLECTION ON YOUR TEACHING SKILLS - JOURNAL

 DAY 75

5: WERE YOU ABLE TO DEAL WITH ANY CONFLICT TODAY BOTH STUDENTS AND PEERS? VERY USEFUL TO LOOK AT THIS AREA WITHIN YOURSELF AND WHAT YOU COULD DO DIFFERENTLY.

6: HOW ORGANISED WERE YOU TODAY, TOO MUCH OR TOO LITTLE? WHAT WOULD YOU LIKE TO BE DIFFERENT AND HOW YOU ARE GOING TO DEAL WITH THIS DIFFERENTLY?

7: WERE YOU ENTHUSIASTIC TODAY? HOW DID THE CLASS RESPOND TO YOUR ENTHUSIASM? HOW COULD YOU DEVELOP THIS FURTHER?

8: WERE YOU CONFIDENT TODAY, HOW CONFIDENT ARE YOU ALREADY? COULD THIS BE BETTER WITHIN YOUR STUDENTS AND PEERS.

9: HOW SUPPORTIVE HAVE YOU BEEN TODAY, WHY WAS THIS? WHAT IMPROVEMENTS COULD YOU MAKE TO IMPROVE IN THIS AREA?

REFLECTION ON YOUR TEACHING SKILLS - JOURNAL

DAY 76

DATE:-   /   /

1: HOW DISTRACTED DID YOU FIND YOURSELF TODAY WHY WAS THIS? HOW COULD YOU CHANGE THIS FOR THE NEXT LESSON?

2: HOW MOTIVATED WERE YOU TODAY, WHY WAS THIS AND WHAT COULD YOU DO TO IMPROVE THIS?

3: HOW GOOD WERE YOUR COMMUNICATION SKILLS TODAY? WHAT WOULD YOU LIKE TO BE DIFFERENT & HOW CAN YOU START THE CHANGE?

4: WERE YOU PATIENT TODAY? HOW DIFFERENT DO YOU FIND YOURSELF WITH DIFFERENT STUDENTS AND CLASSES? THEN LOOK AT WHY YOU MAY BE DIFFERENT?

REFLECTION ON YOUR TEACHING SKILLS - JOURNAL

 DAY 76

5: WERE YOU ABLE TO DEAL WITH ANY CONFLICT TODAY BOTH STUDENTS AND PEERS? VERY USEFUL TO LOOK AT THIS AREA WITHIN YOURSELF AND WHAT YOU COULD DO DIFFERENTLY.

6: HOW ORGANISED WERE YOU TODAY, TOO MUCH OR TOO LITTLE? WHAT WOULD YOU LIKE TO BE DIFFERENT AND HOW YOU ARE GOING TO DEAL WITH THIS DIFFERENTLY?

7: WERE YOU ENTHUSIASTIC TODAY? HOW DID THE CLASS RESPOND TO YOUR ENTHUSIASM? HOW COULD YOU DEVELOP THIS FURTHER?

8: WERE YOU CONFIDENT TODAY, HOW CONFIDENT ARE YOU ALREADY? COULD THIS BE BETTER WITHIN YOUR STUDENTS AND PEERS.

9: HOW SUPPORTIVE HAVE YOU BEEN TODAY, WHY WAS THIS? WHAT IMPROVEMENTS COULD YOU MAKE TO IMPROVE IN THIS AREA?

REFLECTION ON YOUR TEACHING SKILLS - JOURNAL

DAY 77

DATE:-   /   /

1: HOW DISTRACTED DID YOU FIND YOURSELF TODAY WHY WAS THIS? HOW COULD YOU CHANGE THIS FOR THE NEXT LESSON?

2: HOW MOTIVATED WERE YOU TODAY, WHY WAS THIS AND WHAT COULD YOU DO TO IMPROVE THIS?

3: HOW GOOD WERE YOUR COMMUNICATION SKILLS TODAY? WHAT WOULD YOU LIKE TO BE DIFFERENT & HOW CAN YOU START THE CHANGE?

4: WERE YOU PATIENT TODAY? HOW DIFFERENT DO YOU FIND YOURSELF WITH DIFFERENT STUDENTS AND CLASSES? THEN LOOK AT WHY YOU MAY BE DIFFERENT?

REFLECTION ON YOUR TEACHING SKILLS - JOURNAL

 DAY 77

5: WERE YOU ABLE TO DEAL WITH ANY CONFLICT TODAY BOTH STUDENTS AND PEERS? VERY USEFUL TO LOOK AT THIS AREA WITHIN YOURSELF AND WHAT YOU COULD DO DIFFERENTLY.

6: HOW ORGANISED WERE YOU TODAY, TOO MUCH OR TOO LITTLE? WHAT WOULD YOU LIKE TO BE DIFFERENT AND HOW YOU ARE GOING TO DEAL WITH THIS DIFFERENTLY?

7: WERE YOU ENTHUSIASTIC TODAY? HOW DID THE CLASS RESPOND TO YOUR ENTHUSIASM? HOW COULD YOU DEVELOP THIS FURTHER?

8: WERE YOU CONFIDENT TODAY, HOW CONFIDENT ARE YOU ALREADY? COULD THIS BE BETTER WITHIN YOUR STUDENTS AND PEERS.

9: HOW SUPPORTIVE HAVE YOU BEEN TODAY, WHY WAS THIS? WHAT IMPROVEMENTS COULD YOU MAKE TO IMPROVE IN THIS AREA?

REFLECTION ON YOUR TEACHING SKILLS - JOURNAL

DAY 78

DATE:-   /   /

1: HOW DISTRACTED DID YOU FIND YOURSELF TODAY WHY WAS THIS? HOW COULD YOU CHANGE THIS FOR THE NEXT LESSON?

2: HOW MOTIVATED WERE YOU TODAY, WHY WAS THIS AND WHAT COULD YOU DO TO IMPROVE THIS?

3: HOW GOOD WERE YOUR COMMUNICATION SKILLS TODAY? WHAT WOULD YOU LIKE TO BE DIFFERENT & HOW CAN YOU START THE CHANGE?

4: WERE YOU PATIENT TODAY? HOW DIFFERENT DO YOU FIND YOURSELF WITH DIFFERENT STUDENTS AND CLASSES? THEN LOOK AT WHY YOU MAY BE DIFFERENT?

REFLECTION ON YOUR TEACHING SKILLS - JOURNAL

5: WERE YOU ABLE TO DEAL WITH ANY CONFLICT TODAY BOTH STUDENTS AND PEERS? VERY USEFUL TO LOOK AT THIS AREA WITHIN YOURSELF AND WHAT YOU COULD DO DIFFERENTLY.

6: HOW ORGANISED WERE YOU TODAY, TOO MUCH OR TOO LITTLE? WHAT WOULD YOU LIKE TO BE DIFFERENT AND HOW YOU ARE GOING TO DEAL WITH THIS DIFFERENTLY?

7: WERE YOU ENTHUSIASTIC TODAY? HOW DID THE CLASS RESPOND TO YOUR ENTHUSIASM? HOW COULD YOU DEVELOP THIS FURTHER?

8: WERE YOU CONFIDENT TODAY, HOW CONFIDENT ARE YOU ALREADY? COULD THIS BE BETTER WITHIN YOUR STUDENTS AND PEERS.

9: HOW SUPPORTIVE HAVE YOU BEEN TODAY, WHY WAS THIS? WHAT IMPROVEMENTS COULD YOU MAKE TO IMPROVE IN THIS AREA?

REFLECTION ON YOUR TEACHING SKILLS - JOURNAL

DAY 79

DATE:-   /   /

1: HOW DISTRACTED DID YOU FIND YOURSELF TODAY WHY WAS THIS? HOW COULD YOU CHANGE THIS FOR THE NEXT LESSON?

2: HOW MOTIVATED WERE YOU TODAY, WHY WAS THIS AND WHAT COULD YOU DO TO IMPROVE THIS?

3: HOW GOOD WERE YOUR COMMUNICATION SKILLS TODAY? WHAT WOULD YOU LIKE TO BE DIFFERENT & HOW CAN YOU START THE CHANGE?

4: WERE YOU PATIENT TODAY? HOW DIFFERENT DO YOU FIND YOURSELF WITH DIFFERENT STUDENTS AND CLASSES? THEN LOOK AT WHY YOU MAY BE DIFFERENT?

REFLECTION ON YOUR TEACHING SKILLS - JOURNAL

 DAY 79

5: WERE YOU ABLE TO DEAL WITH ANY CONFLICT TODAY BOTH STUDENTS AND PEERS? VERY USEFUL TO LOOK AT THIS AREA WITHIN YOURSELF AND WHAT YOU COULD DO DIFFERENTLY.

6: HOW ORGANISED WERE YOU TODAY, TOO MUCH OR TOO LITTLE? WHAT WOULD YOU LIKE TO BE DIFFERENT AND HOW YOU ARE GOING TO DEAL WITH THIS DIFFERENTLY?

7: WERE YOU ENTHUSIASTIC TODAY? HOW DID THE CLASS RESPOND TO YOUR ENTHUSIASM? HOW COULD YOU DEVELOP THIS FURTHER?

8: WERE YOU CONFIDENT TODAY, HOW CONFIDENT ARE YOU ALREADY? COULD THIS BE BETTER WITHIN YOUR STUDENTS AND PEERS.

9: HOW SUPPORTIVE HAVE YOU BEEN TODAY, WHY WAS THIS? WHAT IMPROVEMENTS COULD YOU MAKE TO IMPROVE IN THIS AREA?

REFLECTION ON YOUR TEACHING SKILLS - JOURNAL

DAY 80

DATE:-   /   /

1: HOW DISTRACTED DID YOU FIND YOURSELF TODAY WHY WAS THIS? HOW COULD YOU CHANGE THIS FOR THE NEXT LESSON?

2: HOW MOTIVATED WERE YOU TODAY, WHY WAS THIS AND WHAT COULD YOU DO TO IMPROVE THIS?

3: HOW GOOD WERE YOUR COMMUNICATION SKILLS TODAY? WHAT WOULD YOU LIKE TO BE DIFFERENT & HOW CAN YOU START THE CHANGE?

4: WERE YOU PATIENT TODAY? HOW DIFFERENT DO YOU FIND YOURSELF WITH DIFFERENT STUDENTS AND CLASSES? THEN LOOK AT WHY YOU MAY BE DIFFERENT?

REFLECTION ON YOUR TEACHING SKILLS - JOURNAL

 DAY 80

5: WERE YOU ABLE TO DEAL WITH ANY CONFLICT TODAY BOTH STUDENTS AND PEERS? VERY USEFUL TO LOOK AT THIS AREA WITHIN YOURSELF AND WHAT YOU COULD DO DIFFERENTLY.

6: HOW ORGANISED WERE YOU TODAY, TOO MUCH OR TOO LITTLE? WHAT WOULD YOU LIKE TO BE DIFFERENT AND HOW YOU ARE GOING TO DEAL WITH THIS DIFFERENTLY?

7: WERE YOU ENTHUSIASTIC TODAY? HOW DID THE CLASS RESPOND TO YOUR ENTHUSIASM? HOW COULD YOU DEVELOP THIS FURTHER?

8: WERE YOU CONFIDENT TODAY, HOW CONFIDENT ARE YOU ALREADY? COULD THIS BE BETTER WITHIN YOUR STUDENTS AND PEERS.

9: HOW SUPPORTIVE HAVE YOU BEEN TODAY, WHY WAS THIS? WHAT IMPROVEMENTS COULD YOU MAKE TO IMPROVE IN THIS AREA?

REFLECTION ON YOUR TEACHING SKILLS - JOURNAL

DAY 71 - 80 REVIEW

1: HOW HAVE I GROWN OVER THE LAST 10 DAYS?

2: WHAT AM I GOING TO FOCUS ON OVER THE NEXT 10 DAYS?

3: WHAT FIVE THINGS AM I POSITIVELY TAKING FROM THE LAST 10 DAYS AND MOVING THEM FORWARD INTO THE NEXT 10 DAYS.

-
-
-
-
-

4: WHAT KEY AREAS WOULD I LIKE TO CONCENTRATE ON TO IMPROVE MY TEACHING SKILLS FURTHER?

> "A great teacher can teach Calculus with a paper clip and literature in an empty field. Technology is just another tool, not a destination."

REFLECTION ON YOUR TEACHING SKILLS - JOURNAL

DAY 81

DATE:-   /   /

1: HOW DISTRACTED DID YOU FIND YOURSELF TODAY WHY WAS THIS? HOW COULD YOU CHANGE THIS FOR THE NEXT LESSON?

2: HOW MOTIVATED WERE YOU TODAY, WHY WAS THIS AND WHAT COULD YOU DO TO IMPROVE THIS?

3: HOW GOOD WERE YOUR COMMUNICATION SKILLS TODAY? WHAT WOULD YOU LIKE TO BE DIFFERENT & HOW CAN YOU START THE CHANGE?

4: WERE YOU PATIENT TODAY? HOW DIFFERENT DO YOU FIND YOURSELF WITH DIFFERENT STUDENTS AND CLASSES? THEN LOOK AT WHY YOU MAY BE DIFFERENT?

REFLECTION ON YOUR TEACHING SKILLS - JOURNAL

 DAY 81

5: WERE YOU ABLE TO DEAL WITH ANY CONFLICT TODAY BOTH STUDENTS AND PEERS? VERY USEFUL TO LOOK AT THIS AREA WITHIN YOURSELF AND WHAT YOU COULD DO DIFFERENTLY.

6: HOW ORGANISED WERE YOU TODAY, TOO MUCH OR TOO LITTLE? WHAT WOULD YOU LIKE TO BE DIFFERENT AND HOW YOU ARE GOING TO DEAL WITH THIS DIFFERENTLY?

7: WERE YOU ENTHUSIASTIC TODAY? HOW DID THE CLASS RESPOND TO YOUR ENTHUSIASM? HOW COULD YOU DEVELOP THIS FURTHER?

8: WERE YOU CONFIDENT TODAY, HOW CONFIDENT ARE YOU ALREADY? COULD THIS BE BETTER WITHIN YOUR STUDENTS AND PEERS.

9: HOW SUPPORTIVE HAVE YOU BEEN TODAY, WHY WAS THIS? WHAT IMPROVEMENTS COULD YOU MAKE TO IMPROVE IN THIS AREA?

REFLECTION ON YOUR TEACHING SKILLS - JOURNAL

DAY 82

DATE:-   /   /

1: HOW DISTRACTED DID YOU FIND YOURSELF TODAY WHY WAS THIS? HOW COULD YOU CHANGE THIS FOR THE NEXT LESSON?

2: HOW MOTIVATED WERE YOU TODAY, WHY WAS THIS AND WHAT COULD YOU DO TO IMPROVE THIS?

3: HOW GOOD WERE YOUR COMMUNICATION SKILLS TODAY? WHAT WOULD YOU LIKE TO BE DIFFERENT & HOW CAN YOU START THE CHANGE?

4: WERE YOU PATIENT TODAY? HOW DIFFERENT DO YOU FIND YOURSELF WITH DIFFERENT STUDENTS AND CLASSES? THEN LOOK AT WHY YOU MAY BE DIFFERENT?

REFLECTION ON YOUR TEACHING SKILLS - JOURNAL

 DAY 82

5: WERE YOU ABLE TO DEAL WITH ANY CONFLICT TODAY BOTH STUDENTS AND PEERS? VERY USEFUL TO LOOK AT THIS AREA WITHIN YOURSELF AND WHAT YOU COULD DO DIFFERENTLY.

6: HOW ORGANISED WERE YOU TODAY, TOO MUCH OR TOO LITTLE? WHAT WOULD YOU LIKE TO BE DIFFERENT AND HOW YOU ARE GOING TO DEAL WITH THIS DIFFERENTLY?

7: WERE YOU ENTHUSIASTIC TODAY? HOW DID THE CLASS RESPOND TO YOUR ENTHUSIASM? HOW COULD YOU DEVELOP THIS FURTHER?

8: WERE YOU CONFIDENT TODAY, HOW CONFIDENT ARE YOU ALREADY? COULD THIS BE BETTER WITHIN YOUR STUDENTS AND PEERS.

9: HOW SUPPORTIVE HAVE YOU BEEN TODAY, WHY WAS THIS? WHAT IMPROVEMENTS COULD YOU MAKE TO IMPROVE IN THIS AREA?

REFLECTION ON YOUR TEACHING SKILLS - JOURNAL

DAY 83

DATE:-   /   /

1: HOW DISTRACTED DID YOU FIND YOURSELF TODAY WHY WAS THIS? HOW COULD YOU CHANGE THIS FOR THE NEXT LESSON?

2: HOW MOTIVATED WERE YOU TODAY, WHY WAS THIS AND WHAT COULD YOU DO TO IMPROVE THIS?

3: HOW GOOD WERE YOUR COMMUNICATION SKILLS TODAY? WHAT WOULD YOU LIKE TO BE DIFFERENT & HOW CAN YOU START THE CHANGE?

4: WERE YOU PATIENT TODAY? HOW DIFFERENT DO YOU FIND YOURSELF WITH DIFFERENT STUDENTS AND CLASSES? THEN LOOK AT WHY YOU MAY BE DIFFERENT?

REFLECTION ON YOUR TEACHING SKILLS - JOURNAL

 DAY 83

5: WERE YOU ABLE TO DEAL WITH ANY CONFLICT TODAY BOTH STUDENTS AND PEERS? VERY USEFUL TO LOOK AT THIS AREA WITHIN YOURSELF AND WHAT YOU COULD DO DIFFERENTLY.

6: HOW ORGANISED WERE YOU TODAY, TOO MUCH OR TOO LITTLE? WHAT WOULD YOU LIKE TO BE DIFFERENT AND HOW YOU ARE GOING TO DEAL WITH THIS DIFFERENTLY?

7: WERE YOU ENTHUSIASTIC TODAY? HOW DID THE CLASS RESPOND TO YOUR ENTHUSIASM? HOW COULD YOU DEVELOP THIS FURTHER?

8: WERE YOU CONFIDENT TODAY, HOW CONFIDENT ARE YOU ALREADY? COULD THIS BE BETTER WITHIN YOUR STUDENTS AND PEERS.

9: HOW SUPPORTIVE HAVE YOU BEEN TODAY, WHY WAS THIS? WHAT IMPROVEMENTS COULD YOU MAKE TO IMPROVE IN THIS AREA?

REFLECTION ON YOUR TEACHING SKILLS - JOURNAL

DAY 84

DATE:-   /   /

1: HOW DISTRACTED DID YOU FIND YOURSELF TODAY WHY WAS THIS? HOW COULD YOU CHANGE THIS FOR THE NEXT LESSON?

2: HOW MOTIVATED WERE YOU TODAY, WHY WAS THIS AND WHAT COULD YOU DO TO IMPROVE THIS?

3: HOW GOOD WERE YOUR COMMUNICATION SKILLS TODAY? WHAT WOULD YOU LIKE TO BE DIFFERENT & HOW CAN YOU START THE CHANGE?

4: WERE YOU PATIENT TODAY? HOW DIFFERENT DO YOU FIND YOURSELF WITH DIFFERENT STUDENTS AND CLASSES? THEN LOOK AT WHY YOU MAY BE DIFFERENT?

REFLECTION ON YOUR TEACHING SKILLS - JOURNAL

 DAY 84

5: WERE YOU ABLE TO DEAL WITH ANY CONFLICT TODAY BOTH STUDENTS AND PEERS? VERY USEFUL TO LOOK AT THIS AREA WITHIN YOURSELF AND WHAT YOU COULD DO DIFFERENTLY.

6: HOW ORGANISED WERE YOU TODAY, TOO MUCH OR TOO LITTLE? WHAT WOULD YOU LIKE TO BE DIFFERENT AND HOW YOU ARE GOING TO DEAL WITH THIS DIFFERENTLY?

7: WERE YOU ENTHUSIASTIC TODAY? HOW DID THE CLASS RESPOND TO YOUR ENTHUSIASM? HOW COULD YOU DEVELOP THIS FURTHER?

8: WERE YOU CONFIDENT TODAY, HOW CONFIDENT ARE YOU ALREADY? COULD THIS BE BETTER WITHIN YOUR STUDENTS AND PEERS.

9: HOW SUPPORTIVE HAVE YOU BEEN TODAY, WHY WAS THIS? WHAT IMPROVEMENTS COULD YOU MAKE TO IMPROVE IN THIS AREA?

REFLECTION ON YOUR TEACHING SKILLS - JOURNAL

DAY 85

DATE:-   /   /

1: HOW DISTRACTED DID YOU FIND YOURSELF TODAY WHY WAS THIS? HOW COULD YOU CHANGE THIS FOR THE NEXT LESSON?

2: HOW MOTIVATED WERE YOU TODAY, WHY WAS THIS AND WHAT COULD YOU DO TO IMPROVE THIS?

3: HOW GOOD WERE YOUR COMMUNICATION SKILLS TODAY? WHAT WOULD YOU LIKE TO BE DIFFERENT & HOW CAN YOU START THE CHANGE?

4: WERE YOU PATIENT TODAY? HOW DIFFERENT DO YOU FIND YOURSELF WITH DIFFERENT STUDENTS AND CLASSES? THEN LOOK AT WHY YOU MAY BE DIFFERENT?

REFLECTION ON YOUR TEACHING SKILLS - JOURNAL

 DAY 85

5: WERE YOU ABLE TO DEAL WITH ANY CONFLICT TODAY BOTH STUDENTS AND PEERS? VERY USEFUL TO LOOK AT THIS AREA WITHIN YOURSELF AND WHAT YOU COULD DO DIFFERENTLY.

6: HOW ORGANISED WERE YOU TODAY, TOO MUCH OR TOO LITTLE? WHAT WOULD YOU LIKE TO BE DIFFERENT AND HOW YOU ARE GOING TO DEAL WITH THIS DIFFERENTLY?

7: WERE YOU ENTHUSIASTIC TODAY? HOW DID THE CLASS RESPOND TO YOUR ENTHUSIASM? HOW COULD YOU DEVELOP THIS FURTHER?

8: WERE YOU CONFIDENT TODAY, HOW CONFIDENT ARE YOU ALREADY? COULD THIS BE BETTER WITHIN YOUR STUDENTS AND PEERS.

9: HOW SUPPORTIVE HAVE YOU BEEN TODAY, WHY WAS THIS? WHAT IMPROVEMENTS COULD YOU MAKE TO IMPROVE IN THIS AREA?

REFLECTION ON YOUR TEACHING SKILLS - JOURNAL

DAY 86

DATE:-   /   /

1: HOW DISTRACTED DID YOU FIND YOURSELF TODAY WHY WAS THIS? HOW COULD YOU CHANGE THIS FOR THE NEXT LESSON?

2: HOW MOTIVATED WERE YOU TODAY, WHY WAS THIS AND WHAT COULD YOU DO TO IMPROVE THIS?

3: HOW GOOD WERE YOUR COMMUNICATION SKILLS TODAY? WHAT WOULD YOU LIKE TO BE DIFFERENT & HOW CAN YOU START THE CHANGE?

4: WERE YOU PATIENT TODAY? HOW DIFFERENT DO YOU FIND YOURSELF WITH DIFFERENT STUDENTS AND CLASSES? THEN LOOK AT WHY YOU MAY BE DIFFERENT?

REFLECTION ON YOUR TEACHING SKILLS - JOURNAL

 DAY 86

5: WERE YOU ABLE TO DEAL WITH ANY CONFLICT TODAY BOTH STUDENTS AND PEERS? VERY USEFUL TO LOOK AT THIS AREA WITHIN YOURSELF AND WHAT YOU COULD DO DIFFERENTLY.

6: HOW ORGANISED WERE YOU TODAY, TOO MUCH OR TOO LITTLE? WHAT WOULD YOU LIKE TO BE DIFFERENT AND HOW YOU ARE GOING TO DEAL WITH THIS DIFFERENTLY?

7: WERE YOU ENTHUSIASTIC TODAY? HOW DID THE CLASS RESPOND TO YOUR ENTHUSIASM? HOW COULD YOU DEVELOP THIS FURTHER?

8: WERE YOU CONFIDENT TODAY, HOW CONFIDENT ARE YOU ALREADY? COULD THIS BE BETTER WITHIN YOUR STUDENTS AND PEERS.

9: HOW SUPPORTIVE HAVE YOU BEEN TODAY, WHY WAS THIS? WHAT IMPROVEMENTS COULD YOU MAKE TO IMPROVE IN THIS AREA?

REFLECTION ON YOUR TEACHING SKILLS - JOURNAL

DAY 87

DATE:- / /

1: HOW DISTRACTED DID YOU FIND YOURSELF TODAY WHY WAS THIS? HOW COULD YOU CHANGE THIS FOR THE NEXT LESSON?

2: HOW MOTIVATED WERE YOU TODAY, WHY WAS THIS AND WHAT COULD YOU DO TO IMPROVE THIS?

3: HOW GOOD WERE YOUR COMMUNICATION SKILLS TODAY? WHAT WOULD YOU LIKE TO BE DIFFERENT & HOW CAN YOU START THE CHANGE?

4: WERE YOU PATIENT TODAY? HOW DIFFERENT DO YOU FIND YOURSELF WITH DIFFERENT STUDENTS AND CLASSES? THEN LOOK AT WHY YOU MAY BE DIFFERENT?

REFLECTION ON YOUR TEACHING SKILLS - JOURNAL

 DAY 87

5: WERE YOU ABLE TO DEAL WITH ANY CONFLICT TODAY BOTH STUDENTS AND PEERS? VERY USEFUL TO LOOK AT THIS AREA WITHIN YOURSELF AND WHAT YOU COULD DO DIFFERENTLY.

6: HOW ORGANISED WERE YOU TODAY, TOO MUCH OR TOO LITTLE? WHAT WOULD YOU LIKE TO BE DIFFERENT AND HOW YOU ARE GOING TO DEAL WITH THIS DIFFERENTLY?

7: WERE YOU ENTHUSIASTIC TODAY? HOW DID THE CLASS RESPOND TO YOUR ENTHUSIASM? HOW COULD YOU DEVELOP THIS FURTHER?

8: WERE YOU CONFIDENT TODAY, HOW CONFIDENT ARE YOU ALREADY? COULD THIS BE BETTER WITHIN YOUR STUDENTS AND PEERS.

9: HOW SUPPORTIVE HAVE YOU BEEN TODAY, WHY WAS THIS? WHAT IMPROVEMENTS COULD YOU MAKE TO IMPROVE IN THIS AREA?

REFLECTION ON YOUR TEACHING SKILLS - JOURNAL

DAY 88

DATE:-   /   /

1: HOW DISTRACTED DID YOU FIND YOURSELF TODAY WHY WAS THIS? HOW COULD YOU CHANGE THIS FOR THE NEXT LESSON?

2: HOW MOTIVATED WERE YOU TODAY, WHY WAS THIS AND WHAT COULD YOU DO TO IMPROVE THIS?

3: HOW GOOD WERE YOUR COMMUNICATION SKILLS TODAY? WHAT WOULD YOU LIKE TO BE DIFFERENT & HOW CAN YOU START THE CHANGE?

4: WERE YOU PATIENT TODAY? HOW DIFFERENT DO YOU FIND YOURSELF WITH DIFFERENT STUDENTS AND CLASSES? THEN LOOK AT WHY YOU MAY BE DIFFERENT?

REFLECTION ON YOUR TEACHING SKILLS - JOURNAL

 DAY 88

5: WERE YOU ABLE TO DEAL WITH ANY CONFLICT TODAY BOTH STUDENTS AND PEERS? VERY USEFUL TO LOOK AT THIS AREA WITHIN YOURSELF AND WHAT YOU COULD DO DIFFERENTLY.

6: HOW ORGANISED WERE YOU TODAY, TOO MUCH OR TOO LITTLE? WHAT WOULD YOU LIKE TO BE DIFFERENT AND HOW YOU ARE GOING TO DEAL WITH THIS DIFFERENTLY?

7: WERE YOU ENTHUSIASTIC TODAY? HOW DID THE CLASS RESPOND TO YOUR ENTHUSIASM? HOW COULD YOU DEVELOP THIS FURTHER?

8: WERE YOU CONFIDENT TODAY, HOW CONFIDENT ARE YOU ALREADY? COULD THIS BE BETTER WITHIN YOUR STUDENTS AND PEERS.

9: HOW SUPPORTIVE HAVE YOU BEEN TODAY, WHY WAS THIS? WHAT IMPROVEMENTS COULD YOU MAKE TO IMPROVE IN THIS AREA?

REFLECTION ON YOUR TEACHING SKILLS - JOURNAL

DAY 89

DATE:-   /   /

1: HOW DISTRACTED DID YOU FIND YOURSELF TODAY WHY WAS THIS? HOW COULD YOU CHANGE THIS FOR THE NEXT LESSON?

2: HOW MOTIVATED WERE YOU TODAY, WHY WAS THIS AND WHAT COULD YOU DO TO IMPROVE THIS?

3: HOW GOOD WERE YOUR COMMUNICATION SKILLS TODAY? WHAT WOULD YOU LIKE TO BE DIFFERENT & HOW CAN YOU START THE CHANGE?

4: WERE YOU PATIENT TODAY? HOW DIFFERENT DO YOU FIND YOURSELF WITH DIFFERENT STUDENTS AND CLASSES? THEN LOOK AT WHY YOU MAY BE DIFFERENT?

REFLECTION ON YOUR TEACHING SKILLS - JOURNAL

 DAY 89

5: WERE YOU ABLE TO DEAL WITH ANY CONFLICT TODAY BOTH STUDENTS AND PEERS? VERY USEFUL TO LOOK AT THIS AREA WITHIN YOURSELF AND WHAT YOU COULD DO DIFFERENTLY.

6: HOW ORGANISED WERE YOU TODAY, TOO MUCH OR TOO LITTLE? WHAT WOULD YOU LIKE TO BE DIFFERENT AND HOW YOU ARE GOING TO DEAL WITH THIS DIFFERENTLY?

7: WERE YOU ENTHUSIASTIC TODAY? HOW DID THE CLASS RESPOND TO YOUR ENTHUSIASM? HOW COULD YOU DEVELOP THIS FURTHER?

8: WERE YOU CONFIDENT TODAY, HOW CONFIDENT ARE YOU ALREADY? COULD THIS BE BETTER WITHIN YOUR STUDENTS AND PEERS.

9: HOW SUPPORTIVE HAVE YOU BEEN TODAY, WHY WAS THIS? WHAT IMPROVEMENTS COULD YOU MAKE TO IMPROVE IN THIS AREA?

REFLECTION ON YOUR TEACHING SKILLS - JOURNAL

DAY 90

DATE:-   /   /

1: HOW DISTRACTED DID YOU FIND YOURSELF TODAY WHY WAS THIS? HOW COULD YOU CHANGE THIS FOR THE NEXT LESSON?

2: HOW MOTIVATED WERE YOU TODAY, WHY WAS THIS AND WHAT COULD YOU DO TO IMPROVE THIS?

3: HOW GOOD WERE YOUR COMMUNICATION SKILLS TODAY? WHAT WOULD YOU LIKE TO BE DIFFERENT & HOW CAN YOU START THE CHANGE?

4: WERE YOU PATIENT TODAY? HOW DIFFERENT DO YOU FIND YOURSELF WITH DIFFERENT STUDENTS AND CLASSES? THEN LOOK AT WHY YOU MAY BE DIFFERENT?

REFLECTION ON YOUR TEACHING SKILLS - JOURNAL

 DAY 90

5: WERE YOU ABLE TO DEAL WITH ANY CONFLICT TODAY BOTH STUDENTS AND PEERS? VERY USEFUL TO LOOK AT THIS AREA WITHIN YOURSELF AND WHAT YOU COULD DO DIFFERENTLY.

6: HOW ORGANISED WERE YOU TODAY, TOO MUCH OR TOO LITTLE? WHAT WOULD YOU LIKE TO BE DIFFERENT AND HOW YOU ARE GOING TO DEAL WITH THIS DIFFERENTLY?

7: WERE YOU ENTHUSIASTIC TODAY? HOW DID THE CLASS RESPOND TO YOUR ENTHUSIASM? HOW COULD YOU DEVELOP THIS FURTHER?

8: WERE YOU CONFIDENT TODAY, HOW CONFIDENT ARE YOU ALREADY? COULD THIS BE BETTER WITHIN YOUR STUDENTS AND PEERS.

9: HOW SUPPORTIVE HAVE YOU BEEN TODAY, WHY WAS THIS? WHAT IMPROVEMENTS COULD YOU MAKE TO IMPROVE IN THIS AREA?

REFLECTION ON YOUR TEACHING SKILLS - JOURNAL

DAY 81 - 90 REVIEW

1: HOW HAVE I GROWN OVER THE LAST 10 DAYS?

2: WHAT AM I GOING TO FOCUS ON OVER THE NEXT 10 DAYS?

3: WHAT FIVE THINGS AM I POSITIVELY TAKING FROM THE LAST 10 DAYS AND MOVING THEM FORWARD INTO THE NEXT 10 DAYS.

-
-
-
-
-

4: WHAT KEY AREAS WOULD I LIKE TO CONCENTRATE ON TO IMPROVE MY TEACHING SKILLS FURTHER?

"The greatest sign of success for a teacher is to be able to say, 'The children are now working as if I did not exist.'"

REFLECTION ON YOUR TEACHING SKILLS - JOURNAL

DAY 91

DATE:-   /   /

1: HOW DISTRACTED DID YOU FIND YOURSELF TODAY WHY WAS THIS? HOW COULD YOU CHANGE THIS FOR THE NEXT LESSON?

2: HOW MOTIVATED WERE YOU TODAY, WHY WAS THIS AND WHAT COULD YOU DO TO IMPROVE THIS?

3: HOW GOOD WERE YOUR COMMUNICATION SKILLS TODAY? WHAT WOULD YOU LIKE TO BE DIFFERENT & HOW CAN YOU START THE CHANGE?

4: WERE YOU PATIENT TODAY? HOW DIFFERENT DO YOU FIND YOURSELF WITH DIFFERENT STUDENTS AND CLASSES? THEN LOOK AT WHY YOU MAY BE DIFFERENT?

REFLECTION ON YOUR TEACHING SKILLS - JOURNAL

 DAY 91

5: WERE YOU ABLE TO DEAL WITH ANY CONFLICT TODAY BOTH STUDENTS AND PEERS? VERY USEFUL TO LOOK AT THIS AREA WITHIN YOURSELF AND WHAT YOU COULD DO DIFFERENTLY.

6: HOW ORGANISED WERE YOU TODAY, TOO MUCH OR TOO LITTLE? WHAT WOULD YOU LIKE TO BE DIFFERENT AND HOW YOU ARE GOING TO DEAL WITH THIS DIFFERENTLY?

7: WERE YOU ENTHUSIASTIC TODAY? HOW DID THE CLASS RESPOND TO YOUR ENTHUSIASM? HOW COULD YOU DEVELOP THIS FURTHER?

8: WERE YOU CONFIDENT TODAY, HOW CONFIDENT ARE YOU ALREADY? COULD THIS BE BETTER WITHIN YOUR STUDENTS AND PEERS.

9: HOW SUPPORTIVE HAVE YOU BEEN TODAY, WHY WAS THIS? WHAT IMPROVEMENTS COULD YOU MAKE TO IMPROVE IN THIS AREA?

REFLECTION ON YOUR TEACHING SKILLS - JOURNAL

DAY 92

DATE:-   /   /

1: HOW DISTRACTED DID YOU FIND YOURSELF TODAY WHY WAS THIS? HOW COULD YOU CHANGE THIS FOR THE NEXT LESSON?

2: HOW MOTIVATED WERE YOU TODAY, WHY WAS THIS AND WHAT COULD YOU DO TO IMPROVE THIS?

3: HOW GOOD WERE YOUR COMMUNICATION SKILLS TODAY? WHAT WOULD YOU LIKE TO BE DIFFERENT & HOW CAN YOU START THE CHANGE?

4: WERE YOU PATIENT TODAY? HOW DIFFERENT DO YOU FIND YOURSELF WITH DIFFERENT STUDENTS AND CLASSES? THEN LOOK AT WHY YOU MAY BE DIFFERENT?

REFLECTION ON YOUR TEACHING
SKILLS - JOURNAL

 DAY 92

5: WERE YOU ABLE TO DEAL WITH ANY CONFLICT TODAY BOTH STUDENTS AND PEERS? VERY USEFUL TO LOOK AT THIS AREA WITHIN YOURSELF AND WHAT YOU COULD DO DIFFERENTLY.

6: HOW ORGANISED WERE YOU TODAY, TOO MUCH OR TOO LITTLE? WHAT WOULD YOU LIKE TO BE DIFFERENT AND HOW YOU ARE GOING TO DEAL WITH THIS DIFFERENTLY?

7: WERE YOU ENTHUSIASTIC TODAY? HOW DID THE CLASS RESPOND TO YOUR ENTHUSIASM? HOW COULD YOU DEVELOP THIS FURTHER?

8: WERE YOU CONFIDENT TODAY, HOW CONFIDENT ARE YOU ALREADY? COULD THIS BE BETTER WITHIN YOUR STUDENTS AND PEERS.

9: HOW SUPPORTIVE HAVE YOU BEEN TODAY, WHY WAS THIS? WHAT IMPROVEMENTS COULD YOU MAKE TO IMPROVE IN THIS AREA?

REFLECTION ON YOUR TEACHING SKILLS - JOURNAL

DAY 93

DATE:-   /   /

1: HOW DISTRACTED DID YOU FIND YOURSELF TODAY WHY WAS THIS? HOW COULD YOU CHANGE THIS FOR THE NEXT LESSON?

2: HOW MOTIVATED WERE YOU TODAY, WHY WAS THIS AND WHAT COULD YOU DO TO IMPROVE THIS?

3: HOW GOOD WERE YOUR COMMUNICATION SKILLS TODAY? WHAT WOULD YOU LIKE TO BE DIFFERENT & HOW CAN YOU START THE CHANGE?

4: WERE YOU PATIENT TODAY? HOW DIFFERENT DO YOU FIND YOURSELF WITH DIFFERENT STUDENTS AND CLASSES? THEN LOOK AT WHY YOU MAY BE DIFFERENT?

REFLECTION ON YOUR TEACHING SKILLS - JOURNAL

 DAY 93

5: WERE YOU ABLE TO DEAL WITH ANY CONFLICT TODAY BOTH STUDENTS AND PEERS? VERY USEFUL TO LOOK AT THIS AREA WITHIN YOURSELF AND WHAT YOU COULD DO DIFFERENTLY.

6: HOW ORGANISED WERE YOU TODAY, TOO MUCH OR TOO LITTLE? WHAT WOULD YOU LIKE TO BE DIFFERENT AND HOW YOU ARE GOING TO DEAL WITH THIS DIFFERENTLY?

7: WERE YOU ENTHUSIASTIC TODAY? HOW DID THE CLASS RESPOND TO YOUR ENTHUSIASM? HOW COULD YOU DEVELOP THIS FURTHER?

8: WERE YOU CONFIDENT TODAY, HOW CONFIDENT ARE YOU ALREADY? COULD THIS BE BETTER WITHIN YOUR STUDENTS AND PEERS.

9: HOW SUPPORTIVE HAVE YOU BEEN TODAY, WHY WAS THIS? WHAT IMPROVEMENTS COULD YOU MAKE TO IMPROVE IN THIS AREA?

REFLECTION ON YOUR TEACHING SKILLS - JOURNAL

DAY 94

DATE:-   /   /

1: HOW DISTRACTED DID YOU FIND YOURSELF TODAY WHY WAS THIS? HOW COULD YOU CHANGE THIS FOR THE NEXT LESSON?

2: HOW MOTIVATED WERE YOU TODAY, WHY WAS THIS AND WHAT COULD YOU DO TO IMPROVE THIS?

3: HOW GOOD WERE YOUR COMMUNICATION SKILLS TODAY? WHAT WOULD YOU LIKE TO BE DIFFERENT & HOW CAN YOU START THE CHANGE?

4: WERE YOU PATIENT TODAY? HOW DIFFERENT DO YOU FIND YOURSELF WITH DIFFERENT STUDENTS AND CLASSES? THEN LOOK AT WHY YOU MAY BE DIFFERENT?

REFLECTION ON YOUR TEACHING SKILLS - JOURNAL

 DAY 94

5: WERE YOU ABLE TO DEAL WITH ANY CONFLICT TODAY BOTH STUDENTS AND PEERS? VERY USEFUL TO LOOK AT THIS AREA WITHIN YOURSELF AND WHAT YOU COULD DO DIFFERENTLY.

6: HOW ORGANISED WERE YOU TODAY, TOO MUCH OR TOO LITTLE? WHAT WOULD YOU LIKE TO BE DIFFERENT AND HOW YOU ARE GOING TO DEAL WITH THIS DIFFERENTLY?

7: WERE YOU ENTHUSIASTIC TODAY? HOW DID THE CLASS RESPOND TO YOUR ENTHUSIASM? HOW COULD YOU DEVELOP THIS FURTHER?

8: WERE YOU CONFIDENT TODAY, HOW CONFIDENT ARE YOU ALREADY? COULD THIS BE BETTER WITHIN YOUR STUDENTS AND PEERS.

9: HOW SUPPORTIVE HAVE YOU BEEN TODAY, WHY WAS THIS? WHAT IMPROVEMENTS COULD YOU MAKE TO IMPROVE IN THIS AREA?

REFLECTION ON YOUR TEACHING SKILLS - JOURNAL

DAY 95

DATE:-   /   /

1: HOW DISTRACTED DID YOU FIND YOURSELF TODAY WHY WAS THIS? HOW COULD YOU CHANGE THIS FOR THE NEXT LESSON?

2: HOW MOTIVATED WERE YOU TODAY, WHY WAS THIS AND WHAT COULD YOU DO TO IMPROVE THIS?

3: HOW GOOD WERE YOUR COMMUNICATION SKILLS TODAY? WHAT WOULD YOU LIKE TO BE DIFFERENT & HOW CAN YOU START THE CHANGE?

4: WERE YOU PATIENT TODAY? HOW DIFFERENT DO YOU FIND YOURSELF WITH DIFFERENT STUDENTS AND CLASSES? THEN LOOK AT WHY YOU MAY BE DIFFERENT?

REFLECTION ON YOUR TEACHING SKILLS - JOURNAL

 DAY 95

5: WERE YOU ABLE TO DEAL WITH ANY CONFLICT TODAY BOTH STUDENTS AND PEERS? VERY USEFUL TO LOOK AT THIS AREA WITHIN YOURSELF AND WHAT YOU COULD DO DIFFERENTLY.

6: HOW ORGANISED WERE YOU TODAY, TOO MUCH OR TOO LITTLE? WHAT WOULD YOU LIKE TO BE DIFFERENT AND HOW YOU ARE GOING TO DEAL WITH THIS DIFFERENTLY?

7: WERE YOU ENTHUSIASTIC TODAY? HOW DID THE CLASS RESPOND TO YOUR ENTHUSIASM? HOW COULD YOU DEVELOP THIS FURTHER?

8: WERE YOU CONFIDENT TODAY, HOW CONFIDENT ARE YOU ALREADY? COULD THIS BE BETTER WITHIN YOUR STUDENTS AND PEERS.

9: HOW SUPPORTIVE HAVE YOU BEEN TODAY, WHY WAS THIS? WHAT IMPROVEMENTS COULD YOU MAKE TO IMPROVE IN THIS AREA?

REFLECTION ON YOUR TEACHING SKILLS - JOURNAL

DAY 96

DATE:-   /   /

1: HOW DISTRACTED DID YOU FIND YOURSELF TODAY WHY WAS THIS? HOW COULD YOU CHANGE THIS FOR THE NEXT LESSON?

2: HOW MOTIVATED WERE YOU TODAY, WHY WAS THIS AND WHAT COULD YOU DO TO IMPROVE THIS?

3: HOW GOOD WERE YOUR COMMUNICATION SKILLS TODAY? WHAT WOULD YOU LIKE TO BE DIFFERENT & HOW CAN YOU START THE CHANGE?

4: WERE YOU PATIENT TODAY? HOW DIFFERENT DO YOU FIND YOURSELF WITH DIFFERENT STUDENTS AND CLASSES? THEN LOOK AT WHY YOU MAY BE DIFFERENT?

REFLECTION ON YOUR TEACHING SKILLS - JOURNAL

 DAY 96

5: WERE YOU ABLE TO DEAL WITH ANY CONFLICT TODAY BOTH STUDENTS AND PEERS? VERY USEFUL TO LOOK AT THIS AREA WITHIN YOURSELF AND WHAT YOU COULD DO DIFFERENTLY.

6: HOW ORGANISED WERE YOU TODAY, TOO MUCH OR TOO LITTLE? WHAT WOULD YOU LIKE TO BE DIFFERENT AND HOW YOU ARE GOING TO DEAL WITH THIS DIFFERENTLY?

7: WERE YOU ENTHUSIASTIC TODAY? HOW DID THE CLASS RESPOND TO YOUR ENTHUSIASM? HOW COULD YOU DEVELOP THIS FURTHER?

8: WERE YOU CONFIDENT TODAY, HOW CONFIDENT ARE YOU ALREADY? COULD THIS BE BETTER WITHIN YOUR STUDENTS AND PEERS.

9: HOW SUPPORTIVE HAVE YOU BEEN TODAY, WHY WAS THIS? WHAT IMPROVEMENTS COULD YOU MAKE TO IMPROVE IN THIS AREA?

REFLECTION ON YOUR TEACHING SKILLS - JOURNAL

DAY 97

DATE:- / /

1: HOW DISTRACTED DID YOU FIND YOURSELF TODAY WHY WAS THIS? HOW COULD YOU CHANGE THIS FOR THE NEXT LESSON?

2: HOW MOTIVATED WERE YOU TODAY, WHY WAS THIS AND WHAT COULD YOU DO TO IMPROVE THIS?

3: HOW GOOD WERE YOUR COMMUNICATION SKILLS TODAY? WHAT WOULD YOU LIKE TO BE DIFFERENT & HOW CAN YOU START THE CHANGE?

4: WERE YOU PATIENT TODAY? HOW DIFFERENT DO YOU FIND YOURSELF WITH DIFFERENT STUDENTS AND CLASSES? THEN LOOK AT WHY YOU MAY BE DIFFERENT?

REFLECTION ON YOUR TEACHING SKILLS - JOURNAL

 DAY 97

5: WERE YOU ABLE TO DEAL WITH ANY CONFLICT TODAY BOTH STUDENTS AND PEERS? VERY USEFUL TO LOOK AT THIS AREA WITHIN YOURSELF AND WHAT YOU COULD DO DIFFERENTLY.

6: HOW ORGANISED WERE YOU TODAY, TOO MUCH OR TOO LITTLE? WHAT WOULD YOU LIKE TO BE DIFFERENT AND HOW YOU ARE GOING TO DEAL WITH THIS DIFFERENTLY?

7: WERE YOU ENTHUSIASTIC TODAY? HOW DID THE CLASS RESPOND TO YOUR ENTHUSIASM? HOW COULD YOU DEVELOP THIS FURTHER?

8: WERE YOU CONFIDENT TODAY, HOW CONFIDENT ARE YOU ALREADY? COULD THIS BE BETTER WITHIN YOUR STUDENTS AND PEERS.

9: HOW SUPPORTIVE HAVE YOU BEEN TODAY, WHY WAS THIS? WHAT IMPROVEMENTS COULD YOU MAKE TO IMPROVE IN THIS AREA?

REFLECTION ON YOUR TEACHING SKILLS - JOURNAL

DAY 98

DATE:-   /   /

1: HOW DISTRACTED DID YOU FIND YOURSELF TODAY WHY WAS THIS? HOW COULD YOU CHANGE THIS FOR THE NEXT LESSON?

2: HOW MOTIVATED WERE YOU TODAY, WHY WAS THIS AND WHAT COULD YOU DO TO IMPROVE THIS?

3: HOW GOOD WERE YOUR COMMUNICATION SKILLS TODAY? WHAT WOULD YOU LIKE TO BE DIFFERENT & HOW CAN YOU START THE CHANGE?

4: WERE YOU PATIENT TODAY? HOW DIFFERENT DO YOU FIND YOURSELF WITH DIFFERENT STUDENTS AND CLASSES? THEN LOOK AT WHY YOU MAY BE DIFFERENT?

REFLECTION ON YOUR TEACHING SKILLS - JOURNAL

 DAY 98

5: WERE YOU ABLE TO DEAL WITH ANY CONFLICT TODAY BOTH STUDENTS AND PEERS? VERY USEFUL TO LOOK AT THIS AREA WITHIN YOURSELF AND WHAT YOU COULD DO DIFFERENTLY.

6: HOW ORGANISED WERE YOU TODAY, TOO MUCH OR TOO LITTLE? WHAT WOULD YOU LIKE TO BE DIFFERENT AND HOW YOU ARE GOING TO DEAL WITH THIS DIFFERENTLY?

7: WERE YOU ENTHUSIASTIC TODAY? HOW DID THE CLASS RESPOND TO YOUR ENTHUSIASM? HOW COULD YOU DEVELOP THIS FURTHER?

8: WERE YOU CONFIDENT TODAY, HOW CONFIDENT ARE YOU ALREADY? COULD THIS BE BETTER WITHIN YOUR STUDENTS AND PEERS.

9: HOW SUPPORTIVE HAVE YOU BEEN TODAY, WHY WAS THIS? WHAT IMPROVEMENTS COULD YOU MAKE TO IMPROVE IN THIS AREA?

REFLECTION ON YOUR TEACHING SKILLS - JOURNAL

DAY 99

DATE:-   /   /

1: HOW DISTRACTED DID YOU FIND YOURSELF TODAY WHY WAS THIS? HOW COULD YOU CHANGE THIS FOR THE NEXT LESSON?

2: HOW MOTIVATED WERE YOU TODAY, WHY WAS THIS AND WHAT COULD YOU DO TO IMPROVE THIS?

3: HOW GOOD WERE YOUR COMMUNICATION SKILLS TODAY? WHAT WOULD YOU LIKE TO BE DIFFERENT & HOW CAN YOU START THE CHANGE?

4: WERE YOU PATIENT TODAY? HOW DIFFERENT DO YOU FIND YOURSELF WITH DIFFERENT STUDENTS AND CLASSES? THEN LOOK AT WHY YOU MAY BE DIFFERENT?

REFLECTION ON YOUR TEACHING SKILLS - JOURNAL

 DAY 99

5: WERE YOU ABLE TO DEAL WITH ANY CONFLICT TODAY BOTH STUDENTS AND PEERS? VERY USEFUL TO LOOK AT THIS AREA WITHIN YOURSELF AND WHAT YOU COULD DO DIFFERENTLY.

6: HOW ORGANISED WERE YOU TODAY, TOO MUCH OR TOO LITTLE? WHAT WOULD YOU LIKE TO BE DIFFERENT AND HOW YOU ARE GOING TO DEAL WITH THIS DIFFERENTLY?

7: WERE YOU ENTHUSIASTIC TODAY? HOW DID THE CLASS RESPOND TO YOUR ENTHUSIASM? HOW COULD YOU DEVELOP THIS FURTHER?

8: WERE YOU CONFIDENT TODAY, HOW CONFIDENT ARE YOU ALREADY? COULD THIS BE BETTER WITHIN YOUR STUDENTS AND PEERS.

9: HOW SUPPORTIVE HAVE YOU BEEN TODAY, WHY WAS THIS? WHAT IMPROVEMENTS COULD YOU MAKE TO IMPROVE IN THIS AREA?

REFLECTION ON YOUR TEACHING SKILLS - JOURNAL

DAY 100

DATE:-   /   /

1: HOW DISTRACTED DID YOU FIND YOURSELF TODAY WHY WAS THIS? HOW COULD YOU CHANGE THIS FOR THE NEXT LESSON?

2: HOW MOTIVATED WERE YOU TODAY, WHY WAS THIS AND WHAT COULD YOU DO TO IMPROVE THIS?

3: HOW GOOD WERE YOUR COMMUNICATION SKILLS TODAY? WHAT WOULD YOU LIKE TO BE DIFFERENT & HOW CAN YOU START THE CHANGE?

4: WERE YOU PATIENT TODAY? HOW DIFFERENT DO YOU FIND YOURSELF WITH DIFFERENT STUDENTS AND CLASSES? THEN LOOK AT WHY YOU MAY BE DIFFERENT?

REFLECTION ON YOUR TEACHING SKILLS - JOURNAL

 DAY 100

5: WERE YOU ABLE TO DEAL WITH ANY CONFLICT TODAY BOTH STUDENTS AND PEERS? VERY USEFUL TO LOOK AT THIS AREA WITHIN YOURSELF AND WHAT YOU COULD DO DIFFERENTLY.

6: HOW ORGANISED WERE YOU TODAY, TOO MUCH OR TOO LITTLE? WHAT WOULD YOU LIKE TO BE DIFFERENT AND HOW YOU ARE GOING TO DEAL WITH THIS DIFFERENTLY?

7: WERE YOU ENTHUSIASTIC TODAY? HOW DID THE CLASS RESPOND TO YOUR ENTHUSIASM? HOW COULD YOU DEVELOP THIS FURTHER?

8: WERE YOU CONFIDENT TODAY, HOW CONFIDENT ARE YOU ALREADY? COULD THIS BE BETTER WITHIN YOUR STUDENTS AND PEERS.

9: HOW SUPPORTIVE HAVE YOU BEEN TODAY, WHY WAS THIS? WHAT IMPROVEMENTS COULD YOU MAKE TO IMPROVE IN THIS AREA?

REFLECTION ON YOUR TEACHING SKILLS - JOURNAL

DAY 91 - 100 REVIEW

1: HOW HAVE I GROWN OVER THE LAST 10 DAYS?

2: WHAT AM I GOING TO FOCUS ON OVER THE NEXT 10 DAYS?

3: WHAT FIVE THINGS AM I POSITIVELY TAKING FROM THE LAST 10 DAYS AND MOVING THEM FORWARD INTO THE NEXT 10 DAYS.

-
-
-
-
-

4: WHAT KEY AREAS WOULD I LIKE TO CONCENTRATE ON TO IMPROVE MY TEACHING SKILLS FURTHER?

Day 100
Congratulations

Congratulations on achieving 100 days. You have completed and reflected on your teaching and have created some very positive actions. You have our permission to give yourself an award for achieving this fantastic milestone. Now think about how you can take this forward and grow further, amazing stuff.

WHAT HAVE I LEARNT AND HOW AM I GOING TO IMPLEMENT THIS IN THE FUTURE

WRITE FIVE THINGS THAT YOU HAVE BECOME MUCH MORE AWARE OF. THE JOURNAL HAS GIVEN YOU LITTLE SPACES TO WRITE KEY THINGS DOWN, OBVIOUSLY THE GREATER THE REFLECTION THE MORE YOU IMPROVE. THE PROBLEM IS NOT EVERYONE IS AWARE WRITING DOWN WORKS, THIS JOURNAL KEEPS IT EASY FOR YOU.

GOOD LUCK WITH MOVING FORWARD, BE PROUD OF YOURSELF.

1..

2..

3..

4..

5..

If you have enjoyed this journal please leave us a review on Amazon.

NOTES

NOTES

JCRM JOURNALS
MEET THE AUTHORS

www.jcrmjournals.com

RALPH MOODY

Ralph believes that lifelong learning is precisely that, and should not be limited by age or perceived ability. He has a belief that all of us have the potential to do anything if we put our minds to it. Armed with the right skills, knowledge and attitude, we can all perform to the highest standards. Moreover, his philosophy is that limiting belief is what holds the majority of people back and that, with appropriate coaching, mentoring and training, we can all achieve anything. With over 30 years of training experience, he specialises in trainer, management and leadership development.

> *"Life is a gift and we all have a responsibility to make the most of it, so that when we look back, we know it wasn't wasted"*
>
> RALPH MOODY

CLAIRE MOODY

Claire is an extremely experienced trainer and coach at Target Training, and you can always guarantee she will deliver outstanding results: she is incredibly passionate about both her training and coaching. She has over 35 years' experience in training, coaching and quality assurance roles, with experience as a teacher and in Train the Trainer, working with international clients. Moreover, she has expertise in the management of trainer inductions, standardisation and quality assurance for corporate clients. She holds an MSc in executive coaching and is accredited by Ashridge, a world leader in executive coach training and development. Additionally, she specialises in psychometric assessment, including MBTI.

> *"It's not about being the best, it's about being the best you can be"*
>
> CLAIRE MOODY

HAVE QUESTIONS?

Target Training Associates
107 Cheapside, London, EC2V 6DN
0800 302 9244
info@targettrg.co.uk
www.targettrg.co.uk
www.jcrmjournals.com

SOME OTHER TITLES IN THE JOURNAL SERIES

Coaching Journal
Training Journal
Being Positive Journal
Improve Self-Esteem Journal
Do I or don't I deal with conflict Journal
Action Planning Journal
Management Journal
Rainbow Foods Journal

Contact us for a quote for a bespoke journal for your particular organisation

Made in the USA
Middletown, DE
26 June 2020